LEARNiNG THEORiES FOR EVERYDAY TEACHiNG

LEARNING THEORIES FOR EVERYDAY TEACHING

CAROL THOMPSON AND
LYDIA SPENCELEY

Learning Matters
An imprint of SAGE Publications Ltd
1 Oliver's Yard
55 City Road
London EC1Y 1SP

SAGE Publications Inc.
2455 Teller Road
Thousand Oaks, California 91320

SAGE Publications India Pvt Ltd
B 1/I 1 Mohan Cooperative Industrial Area
Mathura Road
New Delhi 110 044

SAGE Publications Asia-Pacific Pte Ltd
3 Church Street
#10-04 Samsung Hub
Singapore 049483

Editor: Amy Thornton
Senior project editor: Chris Marke
Project management: Swales & Willis Ltd, Exeter,
Devon
Marketing manager: Lorna Patkai
Cover design: Wendy Scott
Typeset by: C&M Digitals (P) Ltd, Chennai, India
Printed in the UK

Library of Congress Control Number: 2019944399

British Library Cataloguing in Publication Data

A catalogue record for this book is available from
the British Library

ISBN 978-1-5264-6981-6
ISBN 978-1-5264-6980-9 (pbk)

At SAGE we take sustainability seriously. Most of our products are printed in the UK using responsibly sourced
papers and boards. When we print overseas we ensure sustainable papers are used as measured by the PREPS
grading system. We undertake an annual audit to monitor our sustainability.

CONTENTS

ABOUT THE AUTHORS

Carol Thompson is a Senior Lecturer in Teacher Education at the University of Bedfordshire and course leader for the Cert Ed/PGCE in post compulsory education. She has had more than 25 years' experience of teaching and managing learning and is an active researcher within FE.

Lydia Spenceley has recently retired as a Lecturer at Grantham College and course leader for the Cert Ed/PGCE in post compulsory education and FdA in Special Education Needs and Disability. She has worked in various education settings specialising in Further Education and Training for the past 20 years and has a particular interest in inclusion and special needs education.

INTRODUCTION

By the time we reach adulthood we have already learned a great number of things; we can speak, read, write, play music, create art, be physical, emotional ... and so on. We have learned to do these things through a variety of experiences and through this process have created our own understanding of events in a way that is unique to each of us. In a sense, we have 'storied' our experience so that it makes sense.

Teaching can include many challenges that are often underpinned by the diversity of experience we may encounter in any single group. Using stories to introduce information is a useful tool as it offers a way of countering received wisdom and opening up the potential of new windows of understanding. A story can stir the imagination in ways that a lecture cannot. By telling a story we are painting a picture, the detail of which can be contextualised to make it memorable for every member of the group.

This book has been written for trainee teachers about to embark on a career within any phase of education. The book's focus is on the theories which underpin approaches to teaching and learning, and inevitably this involves exploring some abstract theoretical concepts which can be difficult to understand. For this reason, we have chosen stories as a way of illustrating this information, thereby providing the opportunity to place it in a context which shows how theory connects to practice. This is not simply a book about the technical aspects of teaching, although these will be touched on throughout – its focus is on how you can use theory to help you teach and to help your students learn more effectively.

The stories we have used in this book take the form of case studies which represent the thoughts and experiences of a group of teachers. In each chapter we have introduced a new character and outlined the concerns they have about their role. We then explain their development through the lens of education theory in the hope that this adds clarity to the theory while also emphasising the importance of applying this knowledge in a practical way. One thing to remember is that not every theory works in every context – theory should be used wisely and sometimes one theory is not enough; you may need to pick elements from different theories and schools of thought – a sort of pick and mix approach. There's nothing wrong with that – if it works apply it to your practice.

We hope that the benefits of applying theory to practice will become clear as you work through the book and we would definitely recommend that you talk to others about your thoughts on this. We believe that talking about teaching is beneficial in building confidence and expanding ideas and so have included a 'Mentor moment' in each chapter which contains questions to prompt discussion about the chapter content. The intention is that these could frame a professional discussion with a mentor or indeed anyone else who wants to talk about teaching.

So, if you are sitting comfortably ... let us begin. We want to tell you a story ...

1

WHAT IS THE POINT IN THEORY?

In this chapter we will explore:

- what theory is;
- why theory is useful;
- behaviourism, cognitivism and constructivism in the classroom;
- reflective practice.

Introduction

If I had a penny for every time I have been asked 'what is the point in theory?' while I have been working in teacher education, I would be a very rich person. It is usually a question asked by new recruits to the teaching profession towards the start of their studies to gain professional qualifications in teaching. Quite often it's asked at the point of their having to submit their initial assignment for the course when many students struggle to build a bridge between the (frequently contradictory) theories that they find in the books recommended for the course and their own practice. The books can make the art of teaching look deceptively simple and it is difficult to reconcile the theory they read about with the messy, and often frustrating, reality of their own classroom practice.

To be honest, at this point I find it very difficult to give a succinct, meaningful answer as what many of them are really looking for are the answers to two very different questions – 'what use is theory to me in my classroom?' and 'how can learning all this stuff help me to be a more effective teacher?'. In other words what they really want to know is how this thing called 'theory' connects with their practice and how knowing 'theory' will be of use to them in their professional practice. The glib answer to their question, and one that is often found in books, is probably something along the lines of 'knowing theory helps us to become more effective educators' but that really doesn't explain why or how familiarity with educational theory will have any connection with their personal experience of teaching. Like education itself, discovering the point of theory is an individual journey of exploration. It is frustrating, perplexing, enlightening and full of moments of darkness and confusion dispelled by the 'light-bulb' moments of realisation and comprehension in unequal measure. The times when the light-bulb moments occur are unpredictable; they depend on the individual, their context and the situations they experience as they discover more about teaching and classroom practice – but they always happen. To explore the connections between theory and practice, we would like to introduce Sasha. As a new teacher studying for a teaching qualification Sasha keeps a journal. By looking at extracts from this journal we will see how theory can be used to develop classroom practice.

Figure 1.1 Sasha's story

CASE STUDY

Sasha's journal

*Got a new job! Well done me! Made it into 'proper' teaching at a college at long last - I've been teaching apprentices at work how to do their job for years and though I say it myself I am a really **good** teacher. I teach them just the same way I was taught by my teacher.*

They've sent me a load of paperwork to have a look at - schemes of work and lesson plans and the like but I don't think I really need much help - I just need to get started - I just need to teach them what I know. Oh, and they want me to take a teaching qualification, apparently I need to know the theory of teaching - don't really see the point when I will already be teaching, but it's part of the contract so I'll have to do it.

Looking at this journal entry it is clear that Sasha thinks that having an understanding of the theory of teaching and learning is far less important than practical experience. Korthagen and Kessels (1999) and Spenceley (2014) note that there is a strong relationship between teachers' preferred way of teaching and the way in which they have been taught. Sasha's current practice is with apprentices; and as Lave and Wenger (1991) point out, apprentices' learning is normally embedded within the activities they undertake, the context in which they work and the culture of the organisation. Apprentices learn by modelling themselves on their teachers and the patterns of behaviour they observe but Sasha seems to think that this form of teaching will work in a different context – that of a more formal educational setting. However, it is unlikely that Sasha would expect a doctor or a dentist to practise without knowing the theory of how different drugs might affect human beings (rather than just knowledge gained from practice), so why is it that Sasha thinks that theory is less important than practical experience when it comes to teaching?

What do we mean by 'theory'?

Before exploring why Sasha may be underestimating the role of theory in effective classroom practice it's important to look at what we mean by theory. Regrettably, Sjolie's research indicated that at the beginning of most teacher education courses students tend to dismiss theory as being something which was *'boring', 'vague', 'out of touch with reality', 'obvious' or 'verbose nonsense'* (Sjolie, 2014, p741) which had limited relevance to their practice and experience of teaching. Theory is generally seen as a set of ideas or general principles which can be used to explain a fact, event or opinion, but it can also be seen as a set of rules which have the potential to guide action (Dye, 1999). In this sense theories are something which are a form of abstract knowledge, *other peoples' (or experts) thoughts and experiences* (Sjolie, 2014, p731). These are often applied directly to classroom practice which, as Knight (2015) suggests, leads to them being regarded by most people as divorced from reality. Used in this way theory becomes a set of abstract, general rules which can be applied by teachers to either explain or guide their teaching practices. If this is the case then it can be argued that simply using existing theory to inform their practice will reinforce the status quo, leaving little room for change and the development of the innovative practices associated with teaching and learning in the twenty-first century.

There is, however, an alternative view of genesis of theory – grounded theory. Glaser and Strauss (1967) argued that theory could emerge from practice in a specific context rather than through the application of abstract analytical constructs and pre-existing theory opening up a space for the development of new theory. In other words, grounded theory is based on experience, what the practitioner finds 'works' in a given situation to resolve a problem, and which they might refer to in future to guide their actions should a similar situation arise; an approach which leaves room for the growth of new theories which might be more suited to the changing context of education. So now we have two forms of theory: theory which is abstract and deals with general principles which Aristotle described as epistemic theory and that which is derived from practice or 'phronetic' theory. Both these explanations of theory are valid, but neither answer the questions raised by students earlier in the chapter: 'what use is theory to me in my classroom?' and 'how can learning all this stuff help me to be a more effective teacher?' – in other words, how is theory related to practice?

CASE STUDY

Sasha's journal

I've got to keep a journal for this course - I gave up writing diaries when I was a kid, but I suppose I will have to do it. I've survived the first part of the year - bit of a baptism of fire but I've just about coped. Some of the other teachers have been really helpful and told me what to do about the routine stuff. Some of the students seem to be learning alright but most of them don't seem to remember what I say to them. It's their fault they don't remember - they just don't pay enough attention to me when I'm talking to them about the basics. They don't seem to grasp that they will need to know the basic principles before they can progress to the really interesting stuff later. Sometimes they just don't seem to be interested in the subject at all and if they aren't interested why are they doing it?

Oh yes, and I have started my training. Seems a bit boring and that makes it difficult to concentrate sometimes and I haven't learned a fat lot about how I can teach better yet either. She says I have to use quotations - well here's what I think so far. It's all 'words, words, words, I'm ... sick of words' - that's from some song or other but I can't remember which one. As far as I can see it's all about writing things down and thinking about them - as if I've got time for all that!

ACTIVITY 1.1

Review what you have read so far and make a list of the things that Sasha is finding difficult.

One of the things which is probably top of your list is the comment that Sasha makes about students not understanding that they 'will need to know the basic principles before they can progress'. Every subject is governed by theories or general principles which students need to understand before they can grasp more complex aspects. What Sasha doesn't see is that his difficulties in engaging students in learning stem from the same thing – the need to have a basic understanding of the principles (or theories) which underpin effective teaching and learning.

CASE STUDY

Sasha's journal

OK - I'm beginning to get it - well some of it anyway. I tried out some of this behaviourism theory we looked at, going over and over the same information with the students, but they were really bored and lost interest - well that didn't work. It wasn't much fun for me either, but when I was moaning about this to one of the other teachers, he suggested that I used a quiz with a prize of points with them at the end of the lesson. I tried that, and they seem more interested now and it all gets quite competitive when they are shouting out the answer, so I know they know the answers. Now maybe we can move onto some practical work.

What Sasha is describing in this entry is what Knight (2015) describes as students' movement from a *prescribed to owned* relationship with theory. In this case the prescribed theory is one of the theories of behaviourism (Skinner's 1938 notion of operant conditioning in shaping behaviour) which has been learned as an abstract concept, but which Sasha has 'owned', using theory as a form of knowledge which can be applied in practice to a specific situation. What Sasha has also found out is that not all theories work all the time. Sasha's initial approach was to try out a 'stimulus/response' approach based on Pavlov's work in the 1890s by going 'over and over the same information' until students could give the answer Sasha wanted. By changing the approach to better match the situation – getting the students to remember the theory by offering rewards (an approach advocated by Skinner in the 1930s) – Sasha achieved the primary objective of getting them to remember the theory.

CASE STUDY

Sasha's journal

I give up - I made sure they all know the theory, but they just can't connect with the practical work. I gave them a simple practical problem to solve and they couldn't do it! What is the matter with them?

Well, it looks as though Sasha may have reached Knight's stage of *owning* some of the theory of teaching, but the students haven't 'owned' the theory they have been taught. Knight's second stage in the development of understanding theory is the ability to make the transition from the *general to the situated* in its application, a way of using theory to make sense of practice. While it's not impossible to succeed by applying general principles to a specific situation without fully understanding them it isn't always successful. It is very difficult to work out why the principles are not working in practice if the theory which underpins them is not understood. Think about the way in which children used to learn how to multiply in maths; they learned their tables by rote, simply having to accept that $6 \times 8 = 48$. They were able to respond behaviourally (and almost instantly) to the teacher with the expected answer to a simple sum, but they didn't know why $6 \times 8 = 48$, simply that it did.

In the classroom children are now taught multiplication in other ways and by understanding the theory of numbers and the principles of multiplication, they can work things out for themselves. It is much the same with teaching; applying a general principle does not guarantee success, it can guide the user, but success will depend on the specific situation. Through experience in the classroom Sasha is now becoming increasingly aware of one of the major dilemmas connected with theory which teachers and other professionals become acutely aware of as their practice develops – the relationship between theory and practice. Applied without understanding, theory is little more than a general recipe which may or may not work depending on the situation.

CASE STUDY

Sasha's journal

*Christmas is coming, and my Christmases seem to all be coming at once! We covered something called cognitivism on my course, all about chunking things up, building things up logically so that students can see connections between things. I tried it out, showing the students how to do something bit by bit and explaining how the theory fitted and it worked - they actually understood!! Woohoo! They could answer the questions in the quiz and they could tell me why as well as what - brilliant - I **can** teach!*

Looking at this entry it seems as though Sasha has begun to make the move students are expected to make – being able to apply a general theory to a specific practical situation. The important thing in this journal entry is that Sasha is now beginning the process of using theory to make sense of classroom practice rather than simply trying to explain it by applying abstract principles – in Knight's (2015) terms Sasha is beginning to *own* theory. Sasha has begun to problematise classroom challenges – students not being to apply theory to practical tasks – and has worked out that behaviourism, a causal theory implying that one action will cause another, is insufficient. Teaching using only behaviourist principles generally results in students being able to give a response to a question, but not in their understanding of how the answer is reached. As a result, Sasha has begun to introduce changes to the teaching methods he uses. By introducing instructional methods based on cognitivism, which uses logical, step-by-step explanations to show students the links between the different elements which make up the theory, Sasha is showing them how to use theory, or how the principles work to reach the answer.

In the process of solving a practical problem, Sasha is (probably unconsciously) making connections between episteme (theory) and phronesis (practice) using both general principles (the principles of cognitivism learned on the course) and grounded theory (knowledge gained from experience) to solve a specific problem of classroom practice. Korthagen and Kessels (1999) relate this progression to the processes of schema development (Piaget, 1936) triggered by practical experience of Gestalt. Schemas are mental concepts, based on information gained by the individual from previous personal experiences, which are stored in the memory. When a new situation arises, the individual unconsciously refers back to the schema to give them an idea of what they can expect to happen.

Korthagen and Kessels (1999, p9) define Gestalt as *the dynamic and holistic unity of needs, feelings, values, meanings and behavioural inclinations triggered by an immediate situation*; in this case Sasha's initial feelings of frustration and the knowledge that students were unable to apply theory to practical problems formed the foundation for the schema. By analysing the situation and thinking about different theories and their potential results, Sasha was able to add to the schema. Sasha decided to use a cognitivist strategy and demonstrate the logical thinking processes underpinning the principles to make clear to the students the connections between each of the elements. When Sasha found that the putative solution worked in practice the schema was further developed and should a similar situation arise in the future Sasha can refer to this extended schema to help resolve the new situation. As new situations develop, additional elements can be added to the schema as they arise from new (but related) later experiences gained in the practical context of classroom teaching.

CASE STUDY

Sasha's journal

Oh heck – I thought I'd cracked it with cognitivism. The students can apply the theory to a simple practical problem, but they can't take it further and use the theory and principles to solve different sorts of problems. Cognitivism is stressing me out. Endless preparation chunking things up to show connections is so time-consuming and they still don't seem interested. Maybe my lecturer will have some ideas – the course is turning out to be a bit more useful than I thought it would so it's worth a try – bet she's got another theory for me to try. Teaching is not quite as easy as it's cracked up to be!

Figure 1.2 Giving knowledge

Well, it looks as though Sasha's students are making progress, but so far Sasha has concentrated on transmitting information to the students. Both behaviourism and cognitivism regard 'knowledge' as something which can be bundled up and passed on to others – something which exists *as an entity 'outside' the mind of the individual* (Morrison, 2014). Behaviourism perceives knowledge as a commodity which the tutor can give to the student, whereas cognitivism relies on developing the students' mental structures so that they can add the new knowledge (given to them by the teacher in 'chunks') to develop their existing schemas. In the journal entry Sasha states that cognitivism is causing problems in terms of the amount of time needed to prepare lessons and that the students are still not engaging in learning in the way Sasha expected. When Sasha explains the situation to the course tutor, she suggests that instead of 'giving' information to the students that Sasha tries to actively engage the students by trying a teaching method which uses constructivist theory.

Constructivism sees knowledge not as a commodity which can be given to students but as something which is constructed by individuals themselves. At the risk of stating the blindingly obvious, all students are different. While they may have had some common experiences such as attending school or catching the same bus to school, they will also have differences in terms of their social and cultural backgrounds, their previous life experiences, they will have had different friends, have read different books, have different interests, etc. All these differences will have contributed to an individual's personal 'knowledge' of the world and shaped the schemas (the ways that they have of making sense of the world that they live in) they have developed. Constructivism is based on the idea that students will build their knowledge by connecting new information with their previous experiences, adapting their existing mental models to encompass new information. Knowledge and understanding are, in the view of constructivism, things which are intensely personal. Each student will construct them in their own way; they are actively involved in the process of making sense of new information or 'knowledge' and adding to their personal schemas.

Figure 1.3 Constructing learning

As knowledge in the constructivist's view is something which is built by individuals it must be accepted that the learning pathway is neither linear nor uniform. 'Learning' is not a commodity which can be 'delivered' or 'transmitted' to the student by the teacher simply 'chunking' up information into bite-size pieces – it requires the active participation of the individual student. Implementing this theory has, therefore, considerable implications for teaching practice in terms of the teaching methods used by the teacher, the ways in which students interact with the learning process and the role of the teacher in teaching and learning. The teacher must relinquish some of their authority in the classroom and move from the role of the all-knowing pedagogue to that of a guide, moving the responsibility for learning to the student rather than assuming it is the responsibility of the teacher.

CASE STUDY

Sasha's journal

Well – it was a bit of a baptism of fire, but I tried out constructivism on my HND class today. They've only got a few weeks to go so I thought it would be fairly safe to try out a new way of teaching with them. By heck – this constructivism is scary though, because I wasn't always in control of what was going on as the students learned from each other as well as me. I'd always thought that being a teacher meant that I should be in control, that I had to have all the knowledge and pass it on to students but when I set them the problem they seemed to work it out for themselves. The good thing was that it engaged the students and the attention level certainly went up when I started making them do the work instead of them relying on me all the time (although some of them still wanted me to use the chunking it up method). It's a steep learning curve for me but it seems to be having an effect on the students.

Journal entry

It doesn't work!!! Today with my new HND starters was a disaster – they couldn't do it and I had to go back to explaining everything to them and making the links for them – I knew it was too good to be true! Back to the drawing board.

Hmmm, it looks like constructivism is getting mixed reviews from Sasha. Looking more closely at the two journal entries though, it is possible to see some significant factors which will affect the use of constructivism in teaching and learning.

Two of the main theorists connected with constructivism are Vygotsky and Bruner. Although Vygotsky was writing in the 1930s in Stalinist Russia and Bruner was writing in America in the second half of the twentieth century, their theoretical approaches have many similarities. Both agree that learning is an individual activity which can be encouraged by the teacher by supporting learners through the process of 'scaffolding' or supporting the learner to make sense of new knowledge. The teacher initially builds a secure framework of essential knowledge and skills for the student (possibly through cognitive methods). The teacher can then begin to withdraw from the traditional teaching role of instructor and utilise techniques such as individual/small group research projects, or the problem-based-learning technique which Sasha used, to encourage the learners to apply their basic skills and knowledge creatively to 'discover' a process which will lead them to an answer. However, as Allen and Wright (2014, p138) note, *different individuals may construct different meanings in relation to the same phenomenon*. The solution or process that the students develop to reach an answer may not be that expected by the teacher or it may be incorrect; in this case the teacher may need to guide, give hints or lead the learners in the process of discovery learning to enable students to resolve the conundrum. Nevertheless, the onus for solving the problem remains with the learner(s) with the teacher adopting the role of a *more knowledgeable other* (Vygotsky, 1978) to help the learner to move across what Vygotsky describes as the *zone of proximal development* (the gap between what the learner knows and what they need to know).

In working with the HND group Sasha was with a group of learners who were building on prior knowledge of the subject gained earlier in their studies, so they could apply the principles that they had learned previously to the problem Sasha had set. By determining which principles or theories they could apply to answer the problem the students were critically analysing and assessing the value of the theories and principles they had learned. In Knight's (2015) view the students were moving from the level of accepting theory to questioning its validity in practice. The new HND students in the other group, however, did not have this foundation and were unable to work through the problem – a more cognitive approach, giving students information in chunks so that they can build a foundation, was perhaps more appropriate for this group of learners. The degree of control of learning which is 'given' to or negotiated with individuals/groups is also something which has to be considered by the teacher. As Sasha notes, 'constructivism is scary' because the teacher is not in full control of the process and content of learning and it takes considerable courage and skill on the part of a new teacher to experiment with this theory in the classroom while ensuring that the students achieve the desired learning outcomes.

Figure 1.4 Situated learning

Both Vygotsky and Bruner agree that learning is a social process. Students learn through interaction with each other and their environment as well as the teacher, but the level of engagement and meaning-making which students may gain from this type of approach needs to be carefully balanced with the degree of control which is needed to ensure that the teacher's learning outcomes are met. Lave and Wenger (1991) describe the process of social learning as *situated learning* where students participate with others within a shared environment to develop a *community of practice*, learning not only the theory but the practices associated with their subject and the social aspects associated with the community. Sasha has previously taught apprentices and perhaps unknowingly also introduced them into the social mores of their profession by encouraging them to copy the behaviours and attitudes expected within their profession. In engaging students in the learning process through constructivism Sasha is *modelling* (Bandura, 1977), a form of learning which encourages critical thinking and reflection.

CASE STUDY

Sasha's journal

I have to summarise what I have learned this year and relate it to theory for an essay. That's fine, but what I have really learned this year is that I need to reflect on things, think things through and think about which theories will fit which situation. When I first started 'proper' teaching I thought it was all about telling the students what to do and them copying. Now I know that people learn in different ways and that they need to understand what is said to them and make sense of things in their own way. Maybe there is a point to theory after all?

Most new teachers spend a lot of time thinking about the challenges of teaching students and Sasha has made notes in his journal about how these have been met. Sasha's journal is an intensely personal record of progress and change which is (probably) unconsciously based on Ullmann's (2015) six-point model of reflection.

1. *Experience*: a description of the situation, its main points and actor.

2. *Personal*: Sasha's personal beliefs and values associated with the situation.

3. *Feelings*: any doubts, frustrations, disappointment that may be felt about the situation (or the joys, successes and high point).

4. *Critical stance*: analysing and evaluating the problems/successes; questioning any assumptions, making decisions about future action.

5. *Perspective*: thinking about other ways of looking at the problem – this may be thinking about other theories or practices that could be applied in the situation.

6. *Outcome*: lessons learned, new insights into the situation, changes in behaviour or thinking, plans for the future.

These elements don't have to be considered in this order; sometimes in a classroom situation a change to planned teaching or the teaching method needs to be implemented immediately in order to address the situation – something that Schön describes as reflection *in* action. However, this needs to be accompanied later by reflection *on* action (Schön, 1983), when the teacher has time to think about what happened, the action(s) taken and the impact of the action(s), to think critically about how other ways (possibly the application of different theories) would have affected the situation. Reflective practice is the final stage in Knight's view of the teacher's developing relationship with theory – the move from using it to make sense of teaching practice to using it as a tool for critical thinking – and looking at the final journal entry it would seem that Sasha is well on the way to completing this journey. In the initial journal entries Sasha was simply applying a theory learned in class; as the year progressed Sasha began to 'own' theory, thinking about it as a way of explaining situations and teaching practices, actively critiquing some theories by questioning their use rather than simply accepting them and applying alternatives.

Chapter summary

In this chapter we have looked at what is meant by the term theory and why theory is useful in developing classroom practice. We have also considered the practical aspects of teaching by discussing how we can use theory to develop our professional practice. We have also considered the importance of thinking about the things we do in a classroom and the impact they have on the teaching and learning process. Think about your own journey of discovery in terms of theory – where are you on the continuum from accepting to owning theory and what do you intend to do to move towards making theory work for you?

MENTOR MOMENT

Making connections between theory and practice is not always easy; busy teachers just don't always have the time to spend in omphaloskepsis (navel-gazing) despite their best intentions, and rely on 'instinct' or 'experience' to counter difficulties in the classroom. But when they do have time to reflect they can, and generally do, make some connection with the general theories and principles of teaching and learning. Sasha notes that 'maybe there is a point to theory after all?' Think about a recent situation that you have had in your professional practice; try applying Ullmann's model and think about how applying a different theoretical approach might have changed it.

- Are you owning or simply applying theory to the situation?
- What would have been (or will be) the impact of applying different theoretical perspectives on the outcome of the situation?
- What worked (or you think will work in the future) and why?
- What changes would you make to your practice having 'reflected on practice' rather than 'reflected in practice'?

Take the opportunity to discuss your findings with your mentor when you next meet.

Suggested further reading

Knight, **R** (2015) Postgraduate student teachers' developing conceptions of the place of theory in learning to teach: 'more important to me now than when I started'. *Journal of Education for Teaching*, 41 (2): 145–60.

Morrison, **D** (2014) Why educators need to know learning theory [Online] **https://onlinelearning insights.wordpress.com/2014/01/31/why-educators-need-to-know-learning-theory**

Sjolie, **E** (2014) The role of theory in teacher education: reconsidered from a student teacher perspective. *Journal of Curriculum Studies*, 46 (6): 729–50.

Smith, **MK** (2011) Donald Schön: learning, reflection and change, in *The Encyclopaedia of Informal Education*. Available at **http://infed.org/mobi/donald-schon-learning-reflection-change/** (Accessed 28 February 2019).

References

Allen, **JM and Wright**, **SE** (2014) Integrating theory and practice in the pre-service teacher education practicum. *Teachers and Teaching: Theory and Practice*, 20 (2): 136–51.

Bandura, **A** (1977) *Social Learning Theory*. Englewood Cliffs, NJ: Prentice Hall.

Bruner, **JS** (1960) *The Process of Education*. Cambridge, MA: Harvard University Press.

Dye, **VL** (1999) Is educational theory being valued by student teachers in further and higher education? *Journal of Vocational Education and Training*, 51 (2): 305–19.

Glaser, **BG and Strauss**, **AL** (1967) *The Discovery of Grounded Theory: Strategies for Qualitative Research*. Chicago, IL: Aldine Publishing.

Knight, **R** (2015) Postgraduate student teachers' developing conceptions of the place of theory in learning to teach: 'more important to me now than when I started'. *Journal of Education for Teaching*, 41 (2): 145–60.

Korthagen, **FAJ and Kessels**, **JPA** (1999) Linking theory and practice: changing the pedagogy of teacher education. *Educational Researcher*, 28 (4): 4–17.

Lave, **J and Wenger**, **E** (1991) *Situated Learning: Legitimate Peripheral Participation*. Cambridge: Cambridge University Press.

Morrison, **D** (2014) Why educators need to know learning theory [Online] **https://onlinelearning insights.wordpress.com/2014/01/31/why-educators-need-to-know-learning-theory**

Pavlov, **IP and Anrep**, **GV** (2003) *Conditioned Reflexes*. North Chelmsford, MA: Courier Corporation.

Piaget, **J** (1936) *Origins of Intelligence in the Child*. London: Routledge and Kegan Paul.

Schön, **DA** (1983) *The Reflective Practitioner: How Professionals Think in Action*. London: Temple Smith.

Sjolie, **E** (2014) The role of theory in teacher education: reconsidered from a student teacher perspective. *Journal of Curriculum Studies*, 46 (6): 729–50.

Skinner, **BF** (1938) *The Behavior of Organisms: An Experimental Analysis*. New York: Appleton-Century.

Spenceley, **L** (2014) *Inclusion in Further Education*. Northwich: Critical Publishing.

Ullmann, **TD** (2015) 'Automated detection of reflection in texts: a machine learning based approach (PhD thesis)'. The Open University, Milton Keynes [online]. Available at **http://oro.open. ac.uk/45402/1/PhDThesis-Ullmann-2015-Automated-Detection-of-Reflection-ORO.pdf**

Vygotsky, **L** (1978) Interaction between learning and development. *Readings on the Development of Children*, 23 (3): 34–41.

2

THE CLASSROOM ENVIRONMENT

In this chapter we will explore:

- factors influencing classroom environment;
- understanding challenging behaviour;
- embedding positive attitudes and behaviours.

Introduction

Have you ever felt like you didn't belong somewhere? Maybe you have experienced being the 'newcomer' with a group of friends or the 'different child' who preferred reading to playing in a sports team. If you were to spend every day of your life in an environment where you felt you didn't belong, or that you were somehow less important than other members of the group, how might this influence your ability to learn?

The desire to belong has been described as a fundamental human need (Baumeister and Leary, 1995), one which is satisfied through participating in regular positive interactions with others. As a result of these interactions we are then able to form significant interpersonal relationships which in turn meet our need to belong. Maintaining such positive interactions in all aspects of day-to-day life may present something of a challenge, but one place where we do have some influence is in the classroom and for this reason the creation of a positive classroom environment is a key consideration for all teachers.

In this chapter we are introduced to Roger, an enthusiastic science teacher keen to share his knowledge, and through his story we will consider aspects of classroom environment and how these impact on learning. An initial overview is shown in Figure 2.1.

Figure 2.1 Roger's story

First thoughts about what constitutes a 'positive classroom' might take into account environmental factors such as the room itself, the layout, the amount of natural light and so on, and while these are important they should not be the only consideration. We must also think about the social and emotional factors which influence the classroom and, in doing so, recognise that learning is more than a simple handover of knowledge. Learning is a complex process in which we actively participate and through such participation are able to develop our knowledge as well as our physical, social and emotional skills. For this reason, managing the classroom environment is one of the most important aspects of teaching, certainly of creating readiness to learn, and it is the teacher's role to ensure that the classroom is a positive place which generates respect, demonstrates cultural sensitivity and encourages each individual learner to develop their abilities.

CASE STUDY

Roger's journal

I love teaching science - you could say it is my passion. There is something so satisfying about explaining the patterns, the structure, the nuances of scientific knowledge. It is something I find really exciting and I feel lucky to have a platform from which to share what I know. Being a teacher is almost my dream job, the only fly in the ointment is that some of my students don't seem to share this passion. They rarely participate in discussion and look downright scared when I ask them a question. This is a bit disappointing but I won't let it put me off, I will simply win the students over by passing on even more fascinating information.

Factors influencing classroom environments

Teachers who are passionate about their subjects are certainly off to a great start when it comes to creating a positive classroom environment. In the case of Roger there is no lack of enthusiasm and his focus is very much on sharing his knowledge with others. What seems to be missing is simple empathy with how others may be feeling and lack of recognition that not participating or looking scared when questions are presented is not necessarily a request for more information. In terms of the classroom, Roger's focus is clearly set on the content of lessons, not on the other social and emotional factors which may be present.

According to Illeris (2009), we must consider two different processes which take place in relation to learning. These are the external interaction, for example the communication with a group of learners as well as that between learners and teacher; and the internal psychological process in which connections may be made with prior learning experiences, or long-held beliefs about our abilities. Illeris suggests that learning comprises three different dimensions, namely, the cognitive dimension of knowledge and skills, the emotional dimension of feelings and motivation, and the social dimension of communication and co-operation, all of which take place within a given social context. Put simply, the three dimensions are:

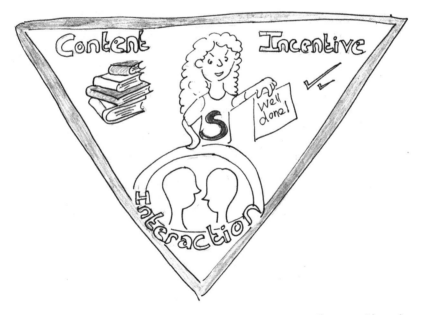

Figure 2.2 Dimensions of learning

* The *content dimension*, relating to what new knowledge and skills are learned. In the case of Roger, this appeared to be a strong focus in the lesson.

* The *incentive dimension* which directs mental energy to the learning process. This includes feelings, emotions and motivation towards learning and may be influenced by previous learning experiences or by how an individual feels in a particular classroom environment. In Roger's class, learners were displaying some anxiety in their reluctance to participate and in their fear of questions.

19

- The *interaction dimension* which could also be described as the social element and includes transmission of information, experience with other learners and interactions with the teacher. In a classroom where the teacher's focus is on providing information, this element of a lesson may be minimised and this was certainly the case in Roger's class.

Within every lesson, learning will be stretched between these dimensions, all of which will impact on how it is experienced by individual learners, yet there is often an assumption that learning is simply about understanding the subject. As a result, the focus tends to be on how to *deliver* the content of a lesson in the most palatable way, sometimes even dividing the lesson into three separate parts as we might when serving up a sumptuous meal. However, the specific way in which a particular lesson is *experienced* by an individual learner will have a significant impact on how it is remembered ... and we all remember a meal that didn't taste good, although perhaps not in the way the chef intended. Imagine being one of the quiet students in Roger's lesson; what would your key focus be? Is it likely that you would be feeling relaxed and working out how this new learning might be put to use? Or perhaps your focus would be on surviving the lesson without looking foolish?

Social and emotional factors in learning both impact on how a given lesson is remembered, so it is possible that even when appropriate teaching strategies have been employed, the psychological and interactional aspects of a lesson could distort the way its content is remembered. Potentially this may mean that intended learning has not taken place at all, or that something completely different has been learned, for example a dislike of the subject or negative impression of the teacher or other learners.

CASE STUDY

Roger's journal

Well, today I decided to take a more interactive approach to try to get the students to ask more questions and show a bit more interest. It seemed to go well. I asked them to create posters which represented their understanding of cells and I set up groups based on their current levels of understanding so that each one would be successful. One or two students did seem to take over a bit and some of them seemed to be coasting so I decided to intervene and make it clear that everyone had to play their part in the activity. This seemed to work as Saffi, one of the quieter girls, put forward her ideas. She was criticised by another member of the group but to be honest this was justified, so I thought it best to just leave them to sort it out. For some reason this seemed to upset Saffi as she ran out of the room in tears. So I guess she is a little sensitive as well as being quiet! Still, the others seemed to enjoy it so I am calling this lesson a success!

PAUSE POINT

What learning is Saffi likely to be taking away from this lesson? Will her focus be on what she has learned about cells or is it more likely to be dominated by the emotion attached to being criticised? What could Roger have done differently?

It is possible that through a different teacher intervention, this particular situation could have resulted in a different outcome. For example, Roger could have provided guidance on how group members give feedback to each other, and the groups themselves could have established rules about how they might work together, Roger could have intervened and provided some positive feedback about Saffi's contribution, prior to correcting any misconception, and so on. There are a number of potential options which could be considered but in this scenario the teacher's focus was again on the content part of the lesson and did not give sufficient attention to other elements.

ACTIVITY 2.1

Taking into account the three dimensions of learning, think about the key factors which impact on the classroom environment and create a list of the main considerations for creating a positive classroom. Against each of the items in your list, add the dimension of learning this it is most likely associated with, for example, you may consider classroom rules as being a precursor to respectful behaviour and therefore something which helps to manage the interaction aspects of learning.

Classroom ethos

Creating a positive classroom environment often begins with classroom ethos. This usually refers to the ways in which students and teachers interact and behave towards each other. Classroom ethos may evolve from a teacher's own values and beliefs about teaching, or from an organisation's philosophy on education and the type of teacher–student interactions that will meet this philosophy. In some cases it may be based on research or general ideas about how best to create environments in which we can learn.

The classroom ethos may be autocratic or democratic, or more likely, something in between the two. An autocratic classroom, where the teacher directs the action, is likely to have strong rules and operate within a given framework, which has the advantage of giving structure and clarity to what happens within lessons. Alternatively, a democratic classroom involves greater interaction between teachers and students and may involve both in decision-making about classroom activity. This has the advantage of encouraging students to take more responsibility for their own learning and for creating a classroom that is a safe and positive place to learn.

PAUSE POINT

What are your initial views on classroom ethos? What are the advantages of taking a more autocratic or democratic approach? What are the disadvantages?

Your choices about the type of classroom environment you want to create may be influenced by a variety of things, for example, your own positive and negative learning experiences, the views of your colleagues, the views of your tutors and mentors. You are also likely to give thought to environmental factors such as the students you are working with, the organisation culture, perhaps the subject you are teaching and any vocational aspects associated with this. Your focus may be on preparing your students for work, for further study or preparing them for life … or all three. All are important considerations and it is worth taking the time to think this through for yourself to ensure that your actions have a direct impact. Clarity is important here as cloudy thinking is likely to result in mixed messages inadvertently leading to a classroom environment that is less than positive.

Invitational theory

Invitational theory refers to a framework of teaching and learning relationships based on the recognition of human capability, value and responsibility. The approach seeks to provide a way of encouraging people to realise their potential by recognising the value of individuals and abilities to work in collaboration. The theory is linked to student engagement and based on the premise that part of the teacher's job is to *invite* students to participate in learning. The theory is founded on three interconnected ideas.

1. A *democratic classroom ethos* – grounded in the principle that all people matter and can develop through participation and self-governance. In practice this would be demonstrated through mutual respect, open dialogue and shared activities. It is a collaborative approach and implies a respect for all people of all abilities.

2. The *perceptual tradition* – which has a focus on individual consciousness and suggests that people are influenced by their perception of events, rather than the events themselves. Therefore, human behaviour is the product of the distinctive ways in which individuals perceive the world and in order to understand why people do things in the ways they do it might be necessary to explore their perceptions.

3. *Self-concept theory* – relates to the system of learned beliefs that each person holds to be true about their personal reality; it could be described as the 'Who am I and how do I fit in the world?' question. This suggests that individual behaviour is moderated by the ways in which individuals see themselves.

Invitational theory may work best in a classroom that has a democratic ethos but it is not necessarily limited to this. The ideas which make up the framework provide a foundation but at an operational level this would be translated into an environment in which care, trust, respect and optimism are the core values.

Prosocial behaviours

Figure 2.3 Prosocial behaviours

As outlined in the description of invitational theory, attitudes related to care, trust, respect and optimism are key factors in creating a positive classroom, and for most teachers these attributes are things they would certainly welcome in their classrooms – but how easy is it to generate an environment in which such desirable attributes are embedded?

Prosocial behaviours might be described as behaviours with are focussed on helping other people. This could include things such as sharing and co-operating with the focus being on how the behaviours help the group as a whole. Although this may seem a little utopian, there are actually examples of prosocial behaviour in most communities; examples can even be found among animals and plants. Adopting a prosocial approach acknowledges that there are positive outcomes for the 'helper' and the 'helped' which include things such as having a sense of purpose or advancing our own knowledge and skills, and of course there is value in reciprocity, in that if we help others when they need it, they are more likely to help us when we need support. Some simple strategies for promoting prosocial behaviours are:

- providing clarity in terms of expectations;

- modelling positive behaviours;

- using positive approaches to discipline;

- integrating desired behaviours into all aspects of teaching;

- using one-to-one support when required;

- fostering a sense of pride in what the group achieves;

- creating a physically attractive and comfortable classroom;

- providing opportunities for discussion (about behaviour as well as about topics being studied).

CASE STUDY

Roger's journal

I have been reflecting on the feedback I received from my mentor who thinks I should give the students more control over their learning. I suppose that makes sense so am thinking about how I can incorporate more of this into my next lesson. My experiment with group work seemed to go well and the students seemed to enjoy the activity. All apart from Saffi who got a little upset ... but maybe she had misunderstood the activity? She is normally an excellent student so might have been embarrassed that she had not grasped the topic as well as she normally did. So I guess that means I have to make sure they all understand future tasks and I must make sure they are aware if they have misunderstood anything. That way they will all have very clear guidelines on what they need to improve and there will be very little room for further confusion! I suppose this means I will have to spend more time explaining ... wasn't this what my mentor said I should do less of? It will be worth it though, I don't want them to be confused do I?

ACTIVITY 2.2

Before looking at the next section, jot down your initial ideas about Roger's approach. What are the benefits of what he plans to do? Are there any potential negatives?

The Pygmalion effect

Another important influencer of classroom environment is the teacher's expectations. Not only do expectations influence student behaviour, they also have an influence on their achievement. According to the work of Rosenthal and Babad (1985) and Goldenberg (1992) teachers' expectations and resulting behaviours have a significant influence on student performance.

In Rosenthal and Babad's research they noted how teachers' expectations were influenced by receiving the results of random testing after which they were told that certain students were expected to learn more quickly than others in the class; these students were labelled 'academic bloomers'.

A further test was issued at the end of the study to see if the academic bloomers had in fact progressed more than the other students and the hypothesis was proven by the test results which showed a significant increase in the bloomers' test scores. The conclusions were used to illustrate the Pygmalion effect which posits that performance is better when greater expectations are placed on individuals. But why is this the case? It is highly likely that we behave differently towards people for whom we have high expectations. This may be demonstrated in higher levels of interaction, the provision of extensive feedback or simply by providing more approval, which may help build self-efficacy. The theory suggests that positive expectations of students influence their performance in positive ways, while negative expectations influence in negative ways: *When we expect certain behaviours of others, we are likely to act in ways that make the expected behaviour more likely to occur* (Rosenthal and Babad, 1985, p36). Goldenberg took this hypothesis one step further by suggesting that the relationship between expectancy and achievement is influenced by both student and teacher behaviours. Student behaviours such as attitude and motivation shape teachers' expectations and in turn teachers' expectations influence student achievement.

In the classroom context we need to be aware of the impact of our expectations on students as, consciously or not, we let them know what these expectations are. Similarly, it is important to have an awareness of how we are influenced by student behaviours, as this will help us to monitor our own responses to them. Within any given interaction we may exhibit lots of cues, such as a head tilt or the raising of eyebrows, all of which impact on the meaning of the communication to the other person. In this case, it makes some sense to think about how we might verbalise our expectations in ways which will have positive, rather than negative, outcomes.

Figure 2.4 Pygmalion effect

Mindset

Mindset is a term which has been used to describe individual attitudes to achievement and is based on the work of Carol Dweck (2008). Dweck suggests that success is closely aligned to our approach to things as opposed to any innate talent or ability. She used the terms *fixed mindset* and *growth mindset* to illustrate this difference. Using this reference, someone with a *fixed mindset* would operate on the belief that their intelligence, qualities and talents are fixed and there is little they can do to change that. In contrast, someone with a *growth mindset* would have the belief that abilities can be developed through dedication and hard work. A simple and powerful concept in the world of education and as a result this work has had a significant influence on teaching practice.

Mindset recognises the importance of attitude and motivation which are certainly useful attributes in helping learners to achieve their goals but it should also be noted that it isn't a magic wand. It isn't simply a case of believing we can do something and waiting for it to happen. We also need to adapt our practical approaches to activities in the same way as we might be adapting our mindset. A positive mindset alone could simply mean we are expending more energy doing the same thing and probably getting the same results; what is required is adaptation in both mindset and method. This means when we are stuck on something, we need to seek guidance from others and try out new strategies until we find something that helps us to move forwards. Simply put, when what you are doing isn't working, then try something else.

This does seem like a powerful tool in helping learners to develop skills that will help them to succeed but how do you actually go about developing a growth mindset? According to Dweck, a starting point is to acknowledge that we are not simply categorised into one type of mindset or another but that we all experience both fixed and growth mindsets in different circumstances and in order to move towards a growth mindset we need to recognise the things which trigger particular reactions. You can do this by reflecting on events and thinking about how you instinctively react in certain situations. For example, what do you normally do when you come across something you consider to be challenging? Do you feel anxious and perhaps want to hide from the situation? Do you fling yourself headlong into it regardless of whether or not you know what to do? Do you investigate options? Do you talk to others? There could be any number of approaches that you may take and many of us will have well-rehearsed patterns of behaviour related to these options.

PAUSE POINT

You are really struggling to motivate a group of learners. You have tried a range of different strategies but nothing seems to work. You are always met with the same level of apathy.

How do you feel about this? What is your most natural response to the situation?

Your immediate reactions to the above scenario may tell you something about your mindset; for example, if you feel that you cannot motivate the group because the subject or your delivery of it is boring, or because the students are impossible to motivate, then you are probably approaching this with a fixed mindset. On the other hand, if you recognise that there might be other ways of motivating the group and are excited by the challenge of finding the right approach, then you are probably approaching this with a growth mindset. However, the important thing to remember is that it is not about categorising your behaviours, it is about accepting the current situation and being open to change. According to Dweck:

If parents were to give their children a gift, the best thing they could do is to teach their children to love challenges, be intrigued by mistakes, enjoy effort, and keep on learning. That way, their children don't have to be slaves of praise. They will have a lifelong way to build and repair their confidence.

(Dweck, 2008, p177)

Embedding positive attitudes and behaviours

Within this chapter we have discussed some of the theory around classroom environment and this will help you to make choices about the best way to manage your own teaching to help optimise learning. It is also useful to consider some practical strategies you can employ to make sure the classroom is a positive place to be. These pointers may be given the general label of 'behaviour management' but they are not simply techniques for managing the behaviour of others, they are strategies for creating a safe environment in which everyone is clear about what attitudes and behaviours are welcomed. In truth, it is extremely difficult to control the behaviour of others – you can only really manage your own responses – but one thing you can do is to set the scene for positive behaviour, which often leads to a virtuous cycle. This works by creating an environment in which everyone is clear on expectations and through positive reinforcement ensuring that these expectations are met. Learners respond to this by behaving in ways which suit the classroom ethos and are effective within the group; when there are deviations from this the teacher manages them in a constructive way. As a result, incidents of 'challenging behaviour' are minimised. That is not to say you will never be challenged again, you will of course … but minimising the level and frequency of challenge will most certainly make teaching and learning easier.

According to Cowley (2012) there are seven elements of positive behaviour management which she refers to as the *Seven C's*.

1. *Communication* – clear communication is essential if everyone is to understand what is expected of them. This means that learners need to know the purpose of their learning as well as their role in it and teachers need to ensure that expectations in terms of classroom participation are transparent.

2. *Confidence* – students want to feel that they are in 'safe hands', so they need to know that the teacher will manage the classroom and the learning. They also want to be taught by teachers who are confident in their subject knowledge, as without this learning is limited. This can be challenging for new teachers, who often aren't that confident about either their subject knowledge or their ability to manage a class and, the good news is, with continued teaching practice this does get better. However, until then you may need to adopt the *As If* principle (Wiseman, 2012). This is based on the premise that we create a desired emotion (or at least the appearance of one)

by acting as if it were real. For example, we can be happier by acting as if we are happier and of course can appear more confident if we act as if we are confident. At a superficial level this does seem to be based on somewhat magical reasoning, but is actually backed up by research so is well worth a try. One way to approach it might be to ask to observe those teachers who appear to you to be very confident in their role. What do they do when they are teaching? What specific strategies do you notice? What surprises you? What do you want to know more about? Most teachers are happy to be observed and would be pleased to answer any questions you might have.

3. *Carrots and consequences* – this approach is based on the behaviourist principles of positive and negative reinforcement. In simple terms this means providing incentives to encourage the behaviours we desire and using these as a reinforcement every time those behaviours are demonstrated. It also works in reverse by implementing punishments for behaviours we don't want to encourage. An example of this is the points systems that are often used in schools, whereby points are awarded for desired behaviours or removed for those behaviours that we don't want to encourage.

4. *Consistency* – if you want to create an environment that feels safe then consistency is very important as we tend to feel more secure when we know what to expect. This is also linked to habit formation; if we consistently do things in the same ways then they become habitual. Taking into account point number three, learners may be aware of the triggers associated with carrots and consequences, for example, if I do this, then this will happen … but if the carrot or consequence is not applied consistently then it will have very little impact. The aim is to make positive behaviours habitual by encouraging responses to specific behaviours. As Cialdini suggests, a simple way of doing this is to use *if/then* statements which provide a simple formula for changing behaviours (Cialdini, 2016). This simply links triggers 'if' with actions 'then'. For example:

   • if I complete this task then I can work on my project;

   • if I miss this class then I will not know how to complete my assignment.

5. *Control* – although you may advocate a democratic approach to classroom ethos, it is still important that the teacher remains in control of activities. This simply means planning, managing time and ensuring that everyone participates as expected.

6. *Choice* – providing choice may seem like a strange option in relation to behaviour management but is effective in encouraging learners to take responsibility for their behaviour. According to Glasser (1998), almost all of our behaviours are chosen and we are driven to satisfy basic needs such as survival, love and belonging, freedom and fun. This theory is based on the premise that the most important of these is love and belonging because of our desire to connect with others. A safe and satisfying classroom environment meets this need so students need to be made aware of their responsibility to make choices about their behaviour in the classroom and if they do so are likely to have greater pride in their learning and exhibit higher levels of self-confidence. Choice can be linked to classroom rules, completion of different tasks or the curriculum itself.

Figure 2.5 Choice theory

7. *Creativity* – if we want to create a positive classroom environment then we need to engage learners … boredom is solid fuel for disruptive behaviour. This may mean that we have to take more creative approaches to teaching and to our use of resources to ensure that motivation is maximised and disruption is minimised. Chapter 9 explores this idea in more detail and will provide some ideas that you can try out in your own teaching.

Much of this is common sense but when we are faced with a group of challenging learners, a calm and logical approach in which we might employ common sense strategies is not always the first response. For new teachers, being put in the position of being solely responsible for a class can be a little overwhelming, but good preparation and the confidence assumed by understanding how to create a positive learning environment will certainly help.

Chapter summary

In this chapter we have considered the things which may have an influence on how learners behave in the classroom. The focus has been on developing an understanding of these factors to enable you to think about how you might manage your own classroom in the most positive way. Which of the theories presented resonated with you? Why? Sometimes learning theories will have a direct relationship to your teaching and you will be able to see an instant connection between the theory and your practice, but this isn't always the case. The links are often more tenuous than that and making practical use of your own learning may require objective analysis of the information presented.

MENTOR MOMENT

In this section we have given starter points for discussions with mentors (or others who may be supporting your professional development). A Socratic approach using questions to uncover meaning is included. The aim is to encourage you to analyse the chapter content and relate this to your own teaching.

- What type of classroom ethos do you want to create?
- What assumptions are you basing this choice on?
- What could you assume instead?
- What practical strategies might you adopt to create the classroom climate you desire?

Suggested further reading

Rogers, B (2011) *Classroom Behaviour: A Practical Guide to Effective Teaching, Behaviour Management and Colleague Support*. London: SAGE.

References

Baumeister, RF and Leary, MR (1995) The need to belong: desire for interpersonal attachments as a fundamental human motivation. *Psychological Bulletin*, 117 (3): 497–529 **http://dx.doi. org/10.1037/0033-2909.117.3.497**

Cialdini, R (2016) *Pre-suasion: A Revolutionary Way to Influence and Persuade*. New York: Simon and Schuster.

Cowley, S (2012) *The Seven C's of Positive Behaviour Management*. Bristol: Sue Cowley Books Ltd.

Dweck, CS (2008) *Mindset: The New Psychology of Success*. New York: Ballantine.

Glasser, W (1998) *Choice Theory: A New Psychology of Personal Freedom*. New York: HarperCollins.

Goldenberg, C (1992) The limits of expectations: a case for case knowledge about teacher expectancy effects. *American Educational Research Journal*, 29 (3): 517–44.

Illeris, K (Ed.) (2009) *Contemporary Theories of Learning: Learning Theorists . . . in Their Own Words*. Oxford: Routledge.

Rosenthal, R and Babad, EY (1985) Pygmalion in the gymnasium. *Educational Leadership*, 43 (1): 36–9.

Wiseman, R (2012) *The As If Principle: The Radically New Approach to Changing Your Life*. New York: Free Press, Simon and Schuster Inc.

3

PLANNING FOR LEARNING

In this chapter we will explore:

- schemes of work;
- lesson plans;
- domains of learning;
- learning styles.

Introduction

A tutor of mine used to have a quotation attributed to Benjamin Franklin on the wall of their classroom and would wordlessly point to the adage 'if you fail to plan then you are planning to fail' when we, as young teachers, were discussing our latest 'disasters' in the classroom, before quietly (and at the time annoyingly) encouraging us to reflect on what we felt had gone awry and why. Telling us that no plan was perfect, and eventually reassuring us that every teacher – no matter how experienced – had experienced a 'disaster' in the classroom when a plan 'went wrong', was little solace to us as new teachers experiencing the disappointment of the 'failure' of a lesson plan that we'd spent many hours preparing.

Failure hurts – but I doubt if there has ever been a teacher who could put their hand on their heart and honestly say that, at some point in their career, they have never had to do some rapid *reflection in action* (Schön, 1991) to introduce spontaneous changes to prevent their carefully planned learning process from being derailed. What they are less likely to remember, however, is the time they later took to think about the reasons for the 'failure' of their plan, working out why something hadn't happened quite as they expected after the lesson. This *reflection on practice* as Schön (1991) describes it (which doesn't have to take place immediately after the lesson is over) lets us examine the lesson in detail after the event – not to carry on beating ourselves up for 'failing', but to allow us to make plans to avoid making the same errors again. By integrating this reflection into the schemas

(Piaget, 1936) (see Chapter 1) that we develop as teachers, we can begin to form the back-up plans that we can call on when we need to retrieve a situation where things haven't gone according to the planned script. In this chapter we are introduced to Ashley, a new teacher who is experiencing a rapid learning curve in relation to planning for learning.

Figure 3.1 Ashley's story

CASE STUDY

Ashley's journal

Well, the course leader has gone off sick and left us in the lurch. Two years in and I'm the most experienced member of staff now. I know it's not their fault but it is going to make life really challenging for me as the curriculum manager has asked me to take over as course leader for now; 'pro tem' is how he described it (had to look that up – why didn't he just say temporarily?), so that means me planning the courses for this year. No summer holidays for me then! It's just my luck that they have changed the syllabus for the BTEC level 2 courses and the HNC/D and staff are already moaning about the new specs. On top of all that he wants me to organise some ruddy community courses which don't lead to a qualification – how am I supposed to plan all this lot for goodness sake? It's beginning to look like 'promotion' isn't all it's cracked up to be!

Schemes of work

It looks as though Ashley is facing a challenge doesn't it? Ashley notes the journal entry that 'staff are already moaning about the new specs'. Most new teachers are provided with a scheme of work (SoW) which has been written by a more experienced member of staff and their responsibility for planning is limited to developing detailed plans for the lessons they will teach. Just like lesson plans however, SoW are not developed in isolation and an understanding of the influences which impact on their development can affect their production and ultimately the formation of the lesson plan itself (see Figure 3.2).

Society is evolving ever more rapidly; the world wide web is less than 30 years old, but today we take using the information superhighway for granted in teaching and learning. The internet age has revolutionised not only the way we communicate but the way the world manufactures and trades. The changes have, in turn, affected the subjects that are taught and the ways in which we teach to facilitate student learning. The changes have put pressure on employers and governments to lobby for amendments to be made to ensure that those in education have access to the relevant skills, knowledge and understanding to eventually gain employment and play a productive part in society. Recommendations from the government and employer bodies (and sometimes trade unions) about adjustments to subject content needed to reflect social or economic changes are referred to by the awarding bodies (BTEC, City & Guilds, etc.) to make alterations to the subject syllabi/specifications. In order to standardise qualifications, a general syllabus/specification (although not the layout or detailed subject matter) is agreed between these bodies. Once the syllabus/specification is agreed, each awarding body publishes a detailed subject syllabus/specification which gives information on content, standards, assessment requirements, etc. These syllabi form the basis for the SoW which are developed by individual institutions, which in turn guide the lesson plans that the individual (or sometimes a team of) teachers formulate.

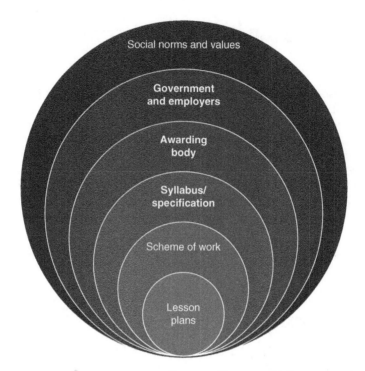

Figure 3.2 The external influences on planning for learning

Looking more closely at the journal entry it would seem that Ashley is going to have to plan for three very different types of course: vocational courses at level 2, more academic courses at level 4/5 and community courses. The vocational courses and the academic courses are award-bearing and will have a syllabus/specification laid down by the awarding body to guide the planning process. The community-based courses however, are unlikely to have a formal syllabus as they generally don't lead to a formal award. There are some generic components which need to be taken into account when planning any course, but each type of course also has some subtle specific elements which must be taken into account in planning to ensure successful learning.

Generic elements of SoW

The generic elements can be thought of in terms of four basic questions about the sort of learning which is required, which will need to be answered as part of the planning process.

- What is the end product of the learning (Taba, 1962)? This might be achieving a qualification, the acquisition of a new skill, the production of an artefact, etc. What will the students need to know/be able to do in order to achieve this, and how will this be assessed?

- What is the process of the learning (Stenhouse, 1975)? This might be consideration of the order in which things need to be taught to facilitate the acquisition of particular skills or traits or the ordering of the building blocks needed for cognitive learning. These decisions can (and probably will) influence the methods that the teacher decides to use to promote learning and the resources that they will need.

- What is the situation in which the learning will take place (Lawton, 1983)? This might include thinking about whether a particular locale is needed to facilitate learning. A workshop with specific tools or equipment might be required for the teaching of skills but a classroom could be a better environment for learning theoretical concepts. You might need to think about whether all the learning will be taking place in one location (i.e., the college or school) or whether some of it will occur in the workplace or on placement, and whether the situation influences the level and content of learning. Students on placement may experience serendipitous learning – finding out about how things work in a practical work situation and what is expected of them in terms of their behaviours, etc. – in addition to the intended learning of linking the theory taught in the classroom with practice in the setting

- Who is going to control the learning process? How much independence is the student going to have in managing their learning? Is one of the course aims to encourage the students in praxis (autonomous or self-directed learning where the student works in partnership with the teacher to make decisions about the learning process)? There is usually an element of this in all planning; however, the extent to which this takes place will vary according to the level of the course and the type of students. You might want to encourage students studying for higher-level qualifications to work independently but feel that those working on lower levels need more direction. Decisions taken at the planning stage in this area will directly affect the role of the teacher in the learning process – is their role to be the leader or do they need to be more of a mentor for the students?

Specific elements of SoW

In addition to these generic questions (which also apply to lesson planning as well as planning for SoW) other important aspects need to be addressed in planning. Padden et al. (2017), in discussing the need for a Universal Design for Instruction, suggest that in addition to these points, planning should also ensure that the SoW is *equitable* – one that is designed to ensure that students have equal opportunity to engage in learning and meet learning outcomes. This could be achieved through considering the need for planned development of accessible class materials and teaching methods as the *reliance on any one teaching style* ... [or single method of assessment] ... *will inevitably result in the disadvantage, or even exclusion, of some learners* (Padden et al., 2017, p6). Consideration should also be given to the incorporation of topics or subjects which are *so important that they have to be included at some level in all the different specialist areas* (Tummons, 2012, p49), such as British Values, Internet Safety or Safeguarding.

CASE STUDY

Ashley's journal

No point in putting it off – I need to get started on these SoW so that staff can start their planning before they disappear for the summer – I'll start with what I know best, the level 2 planning, but it will be handy to be able to work with the staff to help me sort out what needs to come where and when. They're the experts in their bit of the subject when all is said and done and now they've all seen the new specs they should be able to help – in between finishing the marking for this year that is!

Ashley has probably made a smart move in deciding to involve the staff in the development of the SoW; including them in the planning process by acknowledging and using their subject expertise will make them feel valued. It will also encourage them to take ownership of the new course (or any changes that need to be made to an existing one) if they contribute to the planning process. However, while the best course designs can be produced through collaboration, Ashley needs to remember the old maxim that a camel is simply a horse designed by a committee, and that collaborative processes need to be controlled and remain focussed in order to be effective.

Using the new syllabi/specifications for the qualifications as a guide, Ashley and the staff will be able to answer most of the generic questions shown above. The syllabi/specifications generally give guidance on the content, delivery and resources, etc. that will be required. Specific information may also be given on the learning aims/objectives associated with each module or unit together with details of assessment processes (which may involve when and how the assessments take place) and marking criteria. Most subject syllabi/specifications will also give information on recruitment to the course in terms of any prior knowledge, skills or understandings that students will need. Using this information, Ashley and the teams will be able to begin to structure the courses that they will teach into a logical format and plan the SoW.

CASE STUDY

Ashley's journal

OK - the SoW for the new academic and vocational courses are just about there and staff can start thinking about getting the first term's lesson plans ready. The courses are all new this year so there are bound to be some hiccups on the way but at least we have a plan of action for each course now. Well - nearly all - I was alright with planning the SoW for these courses but where do I start with the community course, I've got no qualification, no spec, no guidance to follow - in fact I've got no idea!!!

The need for flexibility

Two things would seem to come out of the journal entry, one implicit and one explicit. Implicit is Ashley's understanding that a SoW is not something written on tablets of stone. Most great leaders know that rarely does a plan (however good and whatever the context) survive its first contact with the reality of a situation. This is particularly true in teaching, where the biggest variable – the students' needs – cannot necessarily be taken into account when planning. A SoW needs to be seen as a working document – something which has a degree of flexibility so that it can (and almost certainly will) be changed to suit changes in circumstances, and students, when it is put into action.

The explicit element in the entry is Ashley's concern about the community course: *no spec, no guidance to follow ... no idea!!!* One of the first things that Ashley will have to think about is the audience for the course. Whereas with the other courses those attending were interested in gaining a qualification of some sort, students on community courses often have different motives. They may want to learn a new skill but they may also enrol into the course for social or personal reasons such as learning how to use e-mail to maintain contact with members of their family.

As with the other courses, when starting to plan Ashley would be wise to liaise with staff and use their expertise in designing the syllabus. Unlike the award-bearing courses, decisions will have to be made about the purpose and level of the course so Ashley can still use most of the generic questions posed above and work with members of staff who know the local 'market' in order to develop the SoW for this type of course. There may also be existing data kept by the institution which can be drawn on to help in planning. For example, if a French conversation course was classed as introductory previously, this might have created a demand for a course at an intermediate level. Attendance at previous 'taster' sessions might be used as a guide for potential interest and also provide anecdotal evidence about the appropriate level for future courses. What Ashley and the staff must remember, however, is the variation in students who will attend. Award-bearing courses which have been planned are likely to attract a largely homogeneous group of learners in terms of ability, age, previous experience, etc. Community-based courses, however, attract a far wider range of students. As a result, the SoW may need to be altered considerably after an initial assessment of the students at the start of the course and some negotiation with the students might be required in order to meet their needs. When planning community courses flexibility is definitely the watchword.

Lesson planning

CASE STUDY

Ashley's journal

Just when I thought I'd got things sorted ... one of the staff - needless to say the one who'd only finished planning the SoW, not the lesson plans - handed in their notice and now I have a newbie to sort out. OK, the SoW is done but while this 'teacher' has trade experience they've never set foot in a classroom. Sounds a bit like me when I first started - I remember how everyone took it for granted that I knew what I was doing. LOL!!! I think a bit of help for them with lesson planning wouldn't go amiss - it was something I really struggled with when I started as it never seemed to work, however hard I worked at it, and I got really down at times when things didn't work. Now, where to start?

The logical place for Ashley to start helping the 'newbie' is with the SoW, explaining what the course is about, its overall objectives, etc., so that they have some context for lesson planning. The SoW can also be used to help develop 'OSI' aims or objectives for the lessons. It will already show the *overall* aim/objective for the course (O), and from this the *specific* aims/objectives (S) for groups or individual lessons can be decided, and once these are determined the *immediate* aims/objectives (I) – the detailed aims/objectives – for each lesson can be set. Setting the aims/objectives for lessons is one of the most challenging aspects of lesson planning for new teachers as the right aims and objectives will help the students develop a virtuous circle of learning rather than fall into a vicious circle of learning (Nuttall, 1982).

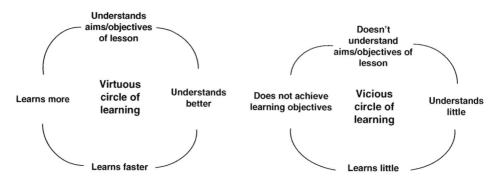

Figure 3.3 Circles of learning (adapted from Nuttall, 1982)

Using domains of learning to guide in setting aims and objectives

One of the first decisions in setting aims/objectives is deciding what you want the students to achieve in the lesson or over a series of lessons. Between 1956 and 1972, Bloom (in collaboration with others) developed the theory of domains of learning, arguing that learning could be divided into three main areas or domains:

1. Cognitive (learning related to knowledge or theoretical learning);

2. Affective (learning related to attitudes or ways of looking at things);

3. Psychomotor (learning related to developing or acquiring skills).

This is sometimes shortened to the acronym 'ASK' – attitude (affective domain), skills (psychomotor domain) and knowledge (cognitive domain) – to make the domains easier to remember. Almost every lesson contains all these elements to some degree, although it may be that one is dominant. It might be that developing an understanding of a subject (knowledge or cognitive domain) is the most important aspect of the lesson. However, in the same lesson putting the new knowledge/understanding into practice by using a piece of equipment, or through the practical application of theory to practice, may need to be included in some way (psychomotor domain). There might also need to be an element of highlighting the importance of developing an associated attitude (affective domain) by working with health and safety in mind when using the equipment or applying a formula to achieve a particular outcome.

Once the relative importance of the domains has been established for the lesson the next thing to be decided is exactly what it is that the students are intended to learn in each domain. Anyone who has ever taught a group of students will be fully aware that they do not learn at the same speed; some students will have learned the basic information at the end of the lesson whereas others will have forged ahead, making links and connections with other things within the lesson or with previous learning. Gravells and Simpson (2008, p21) argue that *Inclusive learning is about recognising that each ... [learner] ... is different from other learners ... The aim is not for students to simply take part in ... [the learning process] ... but to be actively included and fully engaged.*

In order for this to happen, aims and objectives need to be differentiated to allow students to access the information and achieve to the best of their ability. One way of doing this is to use the phrases 'all students will be able to ...', 'most students will be able to ...' and 'some students will be able to ...' in order to introduce learning aims/objectives. For example, on completion of the lesson on bread-making the differentiated aims/objectives for learning in the knowledge (cognitive) domain might be that:

- all students will be able to state the ingredients for bread;

- most students will be able to describe the process of combining the ingredients for bread;

- some students will be able to explain the chemical process which occurs when using raising agents in baking bread.

Determining the verbs (action words) to be used in setting aims/objectives is a critical element in lesson planning. Not only do they determine the aim of the teaching but they can help guide both the delivery and assessment processes. In order to be effective the aims/objectives need to be what Doran (1981) described as being SMART (Specific, Measurable, Achievable, Relevant and Time-bound). This acronym has, however, recently been updated and now not only includes the elements of SMART target setting but also recognises the need for these to be Evaluated and Reviewed periodically in order to maintain their relevance; SMART targets have therefore become SMARTER targets. Look again at the lesson objectives stated above. They are:

- **s**pecific – they state what the student will be able to do;

- **m**easurable – the teacher can check whether they can do what is required of them;

- **a**chievable – all the students will be able to achieve at some level within the lesson;

- **r**elevant – they are all directly related to the subject;

- **t**ime-bound – they can be met within the confines of the lesson.

Once the lesson has been taught the teacher can evaluate and review the relevance of the aim/objective in the learning process.

CASE STUDY

Ashley's journal

Well, the newbie has done a fair job on setting out the lesson aims/objectives but they are a bit limited and Scott is struggling to set the objectives at different levels. Maybe it's time I introduced him to Bloom's taxonomy to help him out.

Not only did Bloom identify different domains of learning, he also identified different levels within each of the domains, each of which subsumes the ones below and increases in difficulty and sophistication.

- In the knowledge domain the levels start with knowledge, and move through comprehension, application, analysis, synthesis and finally evaluation.

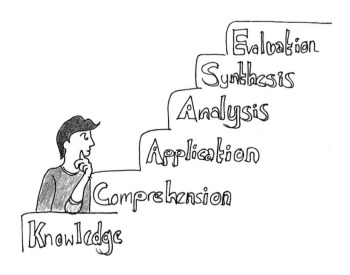

Figure 3.4

- In the affective domain the levels start with receive, and move through responding, valuing, organising and characterising new knowledge or understandings.

Figure 3.5

- In the psychomotor domain the lowest level is the imitation of basic movements, moving upwards through manipulation, precision, articulation to naturalisation.

Figure 3.6

Verbs can be attached to each of the levels to set, assess and measure behaviours expected of the student and the use of the action verb as part of a SMART learning aim/objective enables both the teacher and the student to know what can be regarded as successful learning. For example, if the teacher wanted to develop the knowledge of a student (the lowest level in the knowledge domain) the learning objective might be that at the end of the lesson the student can recall or repeat information. If the teacher wants to expand the student's knowledge of analysing information the lesson objective might state that the student will be able to compare different pieces of information or critique something. In the affective domain a teacher might want the student to respond to information; the phrasing of the learning objective could include the word 'discuss'. In the psychomotor domain it might be important that the student is able to demonstrate a skilled movement; the learning objective in this instance might contain reference to precision in the use of a tool or item or in making something. A word of warning – as you research Bloom's taxonomy on the internet or in textbooks you may find different versions of these levels. This is not unusual as different authors tend to use diverse words to interpret the various stages.

ACTIVITY 3.1

Have a look on the internet or in reference books for Bloom's taxonomy and verbs which can be used for developing learning aims/objectives for each level in the three domains.

Look at one of your lesson plans and see how many of the verbs you have used in your planning. Try changing some of your aims to include these verbs and work out what the impact would be for you and your students.

CASE STUDY

Ashley's journal

Well, Scott seems to have got the hang of setting more relevant objectives for the groups which is a plus. I watched Scott teach the other day as part of a supportive observation and I think he needs a bit of support when it comes to helping the students to learn. I think a bit of work on learning styles might help so an introduction to Kolb's learning cycle might do the trick.

Learning styles

Learning styles range from Broca's (1861) relatively simplistic *right brain, left brain* analysis (which argues that left-brain thinkers learn when lessons are logical, sequential and detailed, whereas right-brain thinkers learn better if lessons are more creative and imaginative in their delivery) to sophisticated psychological analysis based on questionnaires. Over the years, other theorists such as Kolb (1984) have developed the idea that the way in which students learn can be categorised and these categories used to guide effective and efficient teaching. Kolb's learning cycle, a four-stage model, is probably one of the best-known and most widely used models in planning teaching. Initially, Kolb suggests that students need to have an experience, watching a video or listening to a teacher for example, as the basis for learning (concrete experience). This is followed by the student thinking about their experience (reflective observation), and working out what they have learned from their experience (abstract conceptualisation) before trying it out for themselves (active experimentation) – possibly in a different context. It could be argued at this point that there are parallels between this theory of learning and that of the initiation and development of schema advocated by Piaget (1936). Kolb's theory suggests a model for lesson planning – initial teaching which may be direct teaching or demonstration depending on the lesson and subject matter followed by an activity such as a discussion or quiz which will help learners reflect on the information given. This could then be followed by teachers and students working together through discussion or group work to identify the principles or learning that have taken place before students are encouraged, again possibly through group work, discussion or a practical activity, to try out the new learning themselves.

Over the past years other forms of learning styles have become fashionable, for example Barbe and Malone (1981) suggested that rather than learning through reflection and practice as suggested by Kolb, learning could be stimulated by appealing to the one of three methods of learning – visual, auditory or kinaesthetic (VAK). This theory was extended by Fleming (1995) who enhanced the VAK model by suggesting that reading/writing should be added as a learning style (VARK). Building on Kolb's model, Honey and Mumford (2006) adopted a more scientific approach to learning styles developing a widely used psychological inventory test which identified four possible categories for learning. They concluded that some students were pragmatic learners – learning only what was necessary to succeed, some reflectors – those who need to think about the subject matter, some activists – those students who want to 'have a go' at something immediately (possibly ignoring or not waiting for instructions) and some theorists – who prefer to analyse subject matter before acting.

All these theories concentrated on the 'mechanics' of learning and dealt primarily with either cognitive or kinaesthetic forms of learning. Gardner (1984), however, deviated from this pattern, suggesting that learning was related to different forms of 'intelligence'. While his definition of intelligence can be critiqued, he suggested that students, in addition to the accepted visual, auditory and kinaesthetic methods of learning, could also learn through their use of linguistic, logical, interpersonal and intrapersonal intelligences. This move away from the 'scientific' or mechanical view of learning has been added to by Goleman (1996) in his work on emotional intelligence which suggests that the emotional reactions of students to learning are possibly more important than their innate ability in acquiring new knowledge or skills.

Learning styles as guides for teachers in planning learning have, however, been widely criticised, notably by Coffield et al. (2004) who researched the effectiveness of teaching to various learning styles in promoting learning. Nonetheless, it is possible to pick out grains of truth from many of these 'styles'. Many students do learn from reading, others from immersion in practice, others will learn more easily from videos or lectures and, within all of these, there needs to be recognition of the emotional impact on the student of the information itself and the context in which it is delivered. As with all theory it's very much a case of choosing the right theory, part of a theory or a combination of theories in order to achieve results.

Other elements

The last (but not the least important) elements to consider in planning for learning are the resources that are used to impart information and the ways in which learning is assessed. Resources and the development of them is a subject in its own right and there are myriad sources of information available to teachers. Resources are not something that are necessarily tangible such as a video or a handout; they can also include the students themselves and the ways in which they are included in the learning process, something that will be covered later in Chapter 7. They do, however, need to be SMART – specific to the facet of the subject being taught, measurable so that they add to the value of the lesson, achievable so that the teacher has time to make them and the students to complete them where appropriate, relevant in that they need to contribute to the learning process not just be an entertainment, and time-bound in that they are concise and fit into rather than take over the planned learning process. It's hard to admit that sometimes we produce what we think are brilliant resources but they leave students 'cold' and following reflection it may be necessary to ditch some resources that simply don't enhance or contribute to learning.

Assessment is the final element of lesson planning although it is something that needs to be thought about when the aims/objectives of the lesson are being developed. An aim/objective is useful but careful consideration needs to be given as to whether student progress can be checked in some way. The checks might be formal or informal, formative or informative depending on the lesson, but they need to check the level of learning and reference to Bloom's taxonomy is a useful starting point. Again, assessment is a subject in its own right and many resources facilitating assessment are available, but checks on learning must always be relevant, authentic, valid and sufficient.

Chapter summary

In this chapter we have looked at a number of things related to the development of SoW and lesson planning. We've looked at the practical aspects of developing SoW and lesson plans, and discussed the influence that working in the different domains of learning may have on setting aims and objectives in lesson planning. We have also looked briefly at learning styles and the importance of considering the students in the group, the different ways in which they might learn and the influence this can have in creating successful and effective lesson plans. Think about the way that you create your lesson plans and the learning styles of your students and whether you are setting objectives in the appropriate domain to help them learn effectively.

MENTOR MOMENT

Writing lesson plans and SoW is not an easy thing to do. It takes time and practice but, as we indicated at the beginning of this chapter, planning is the necessary evil in order to ensure success in teaching. Think about the way in which you can plan lessons and/or SoW; do you:

- think about the generic elements when you are planning;
- think about specific elements which will affect the final plan;
- think about domains of learning in which you will be working in the lesson;
- think about how you are going to meet the different learning styles which might appear within the group.

Take the opportunity to discuss your findings with your mentor when you next meet.

Suggested further reading

Coffield, F, Moseley, D, Hall, E and Ecclestone, K (2004) Should we be using learning styles? What research has to say to practice. Learning and Skills Research Council, London. Available at **www.itslife jimbutnotasweknowit.org.uk/files/LSRC_LearningStyles.pdf** (Accessed 20 January 2019).

Padden, L, O'Connor, J and Barrett, T (Eds) (2017) *Universal Design for Curriculum Design: Case Studies from University College Dublin.* Dublin: Access and Lifelong Learning, University College Dublin.

References

Barbe, WB and Milone, MN (1981) What we know about modality strengths. *Educational Leadership: Association for Supervision and Curriculum Development*, 38 (5): 378–80.

Bloom, BS, Engelhart, MD, Furst, EJ, Hill, WH and Krathwohl, DR (1956) *Taxonomy of Educational Objectives: The Classification of Educational Goals. Handbook I: Cognitive Domain.* New York: David McKay Company.

Broca, P (1861) Nouvelle observation d'aphémie produite par une lésion de la troisième circonvolution frontale. *Bulletins de la Société d'anatomie (Paris)*, 2e serie, 6: 398–407.

Coffield, F, Moseley, D, Hall, E and Ecclestone, K (2004) Should we be using learning styles? What research has to say to practice. Learning and Skills Research Council, London. Available at **www.itslife jimbutnotasweknowit.org.uk/files/LSRC_LearningStyles.pdf** (Accessed 20 January 2019).

Doran, GT (1981) There's a S.M.A.R.T. way to write management's goals and objectives. *Management Review*, 70 (11): 35–6.

Fleming, ND (1995) *'I'm different; not dumb: modes of presentation (VARK) in the tertiary classroom', Higher education: blending tradition and technology.* Proceedings of the 1995 Annual Conference of the Higher Education and Research Development Society of Australasia (HERDSA).

Gardner, H (1984) *Frames of Mind: The Theory of Multiple Intelligence.* London: Heinemann.

Goleman, D (1996) *Emotional Intelligence: Why It Can Matter More than IQ.* London: Bloomsbury Press.

Gravells, A and Simpson, S (2008) *Planning and Enabling Learning in the Lifelong Learning Sector.* Exeter: Learning Matters.

Honey, P and Mumford, A (2006) *Learning Styles Questionnaire: 80-Item Version.* London: Maidenhead.

Kolb, DA (2015) [1984] *Experiential Learning: Experience as the Source of Learning and Development* (2nd ed). Upper Saddle River, NJ: Pearson Education.

Lawton, D (1983) *Curriculum Studies and Educational Planning (Studies in Teaching and Learning).* London: Hodder Arnold.

Nuttall, C (1982) *Teaching Reading Skills in a Foreign Language.* London: Heinemann.

Padden, L, O'Connor, J and Barrett, T (Eds) (2017) *Universal Design for Curriculum Design: Case Studies from University College Dublin*. Dublin: Access and Lifelong Learning, University College Dublin.

Piaget, J (1936) *Origins of Intelligence in the Child*. London: Routledge and Kegan Paul.

Schön, DA (1991) *The Reflective Practitioner: How Professionals Think in Action*. Abingdon: Routledge.

Stenhouse, L (1975) *An Introduction to Curriculum Research and Development*. London: Heinemann Educational Books Ltd.

Taba, H (1962) *Curriculum Development: Theory and Practice*. New York: Harcourt, Brace & World.

Tummons, J (2012) *Curriculum Studies in the Lifelong Learning Sector*. Exeter: Learning Matters.

4

MOTIVATING LEARNERS

In this chapter we will explore:

- motivation in 'traditional' learning theories;
- motivating through goals and targets;
- motivating yourself.

Introduction

Defining motivation seems to be a complex activity. Is it a drive that moves us towards a particular action? Is it something based on desire ... or maybe fear? Could it also be a product of environmental factors? Or perhaps an innate ability resulting in some people being more or less motivated depending on their motivation skill level?

The word 'motivation' derives from 'motive' which closely links to the needs and wants of individuals, suggesting that we may be driven to satisfy these drivers. But motives can in themselves be determined by desire or fear, so our motivation could be both physical and psychological. At the same time, our motives could be guided by our culture, reflecting those wants and needs acquired through external influences. There are many theories of motivation that attempt to answer these questions, each with a slightly different perspective, and we will explore these in relation to their relevance to teaching and learning.

In this chapter we are introduced to Devi, a high achiever and highly motivated teacher. Throughout her own education, Devi believed in the importance of working hard in order to achieve the best outcome in every endeavour. She is a dedicated teacher who is always thoroughly prepared for her lessons. This approach has stood her in good stead in most aspects of her life but appears to be having limited impact on her students, who seem far less motivated than she is. We will explore Devi's journey through the lens of motivation theory and teaching practice. An overview is included in Figure 4.1.

Figure 4.1 Devi's story

— CASE STUDY —

Devi's journal

I was so excited by the prospect of teaching English and particularly literature. Who doesn't enjoy stories? I was so confident I could instil a love of reading in my students. I had imagined lessons where we discussed books, explored the ideas in them, developed new insights … instead I just seem to be met with a wall of resistance! A sea of sullen faces greets me every time I suggest that they actually open up a book instead of sitting in front of a computer or playing on their phones. How can they say it's boring? And if anyone says 'is this in the exam?' one more time I will scream!

I really want them to be motivated about reading so I am not giving up. My mentor suggested I try a 'carrot and stick' approach which would involve offering some sort of incentive for students to read or some form of punishment for those who didn't. This actually seems like a good idea. I could devise a system of sanctions and rewards; surely that will motivate them?

Traditional theories of motivation

The range of definitions available on the subject of motivation is an indicator not only of how challenging the concept is to define, but also of the difficulties associated with finding specific strategies which will motivate. As outlined in the introduction, motivation can be physical, psychological and cultural and if we add to this 'individual', it is little wonder that teachers have difficulty in finding a 'one-size-fits-all' approach to motivating learners. The different schools of thought on the subject have been grouped here according to their association to traditional learning theories and provide us with a starting point for understanding different approaches that may be used in a learning environment.

Behaviourist theories

Behaviourist approaches are connected to the use of extrinsic rewards or punishments deployed to encourage desired behaviours, some of which have already been outlined in Chapter 1 where we explored the work of Pavlov and Skinner. The 'carrot and stick' method is a clear example of this. It is based on the metaphor of encouraging a donkey to do our bidding through the use of a carrot dangled just out of reach in front of its nose, which the donkey makes an effort to move towards. If the donkey is not motivated by the potential reward of a carrot, the stick is applied to its rump as a form of punishment. Although this is a simplistic approach it links closely to ideas of operant and classical conditioning which are based on the understanding that we form an association between certain stimuli and specific responses. Operant and classical conditioning are both forms of associative learning in that certain triggers generate particular actions. The main differences between the two theories are that *operant conditioning* relates to behaviours that are conditioned through the use of reinforcement *via reward and punishment* whereas *classical conditioning* accepts that some learning can be *involuntary, yet still responds to triggers*. Both occur in our daily lives, often just outside of our awareness. At school I remember being told to stand whenever the head teacher came into the room. Eventually the appearance of the head meant that everyone stood automatically without being told to do so. We had learned to associate the sight of the head teacher with that specific response and we knew that there would be a punishment if we didn't do as expected. We were also taught to respond to the sound of a bell in the hallways and a whistle in the playground, both indicating the end of one school-day phase and the beginning of another. In this way, learners are 'motivated' to follow rules and guidelines about behaviour which may be associated with particular rewards or sanctions. To be an effective motivator, this approach requires consistency in its application as well as a general acceptance of the overall 'rules'.

Classical conditioning, also based on an association between a stimulus and a given response, differs in that responses are not reinforced by the use of sanctions or rewards. It could be argued that in classical conditioning behaviours are *learned* whereas in operant conditioning they are *taught*. A subtle but important difference when it comes to the classroom. Classical conditioning can present itself in negative and positive ways. It may become a form of aversion. For example, if a child had been humiliated in a science lesson, they may have generated a dislike for the subject or felt that they had no ability in relation to science. Or it can be the result of engendering certain behaviours through repetition and reinforcement. A typical example of this is when a teacher raises his or her hand in order to get the class to quieten down and focus on her. Initially the action would not be anything of note but when the technique is applied consistently it produces an automatic response. In this way a specific response (quiet and focus) is associated with a particular stimulus (the raising of a hand); the link is based on repetition and reinforcement but has not been accompanied by rewards or sanctions. Through repetition, students have been motivated to exhibit behaviours that may result in a positive outcome or steer away from a negative one.

CASE STUDY

Devi's journal

I have spent several hours devising my new rewards scheme; it took me weeks to get it right but I am really excited about trying it out with my groups. I want the approach to be more carrot than stick so I have created a system of points whereby students can collect a point for each positive behaviour. They can be rewarded for doing set readings for homework, making a contribution in class, helping others to form their ideas and so on. But I need some balance so I will also remove points if homework isn't completed or the students don't participate in discussion. At the end of each week we will add up the points and the winner will get a prize. I have already thought of some ideas for prizes ... they should be things that are inspiring like books or notepads. It will be great!

One key area of consideration when using sanctions and rewards as motivators is the perceived value of the rewards being offered. Devi has chosen something which she might have valued as a student (books and notepads) but given that her own students have shown no real interest in reading, are these things likely to motivate them? Devi's idea certainly employs the carrot and stick method and is something that the students would become accustomed to if it were reinforced consistently, but is it likely to motivate the students in the way Devi hopes?

Cognitivist theories

There are several motivation theories that trace their roots to cognitive processes of learning and have their basis in the ways in which individuals make sense of the information they are presented with. Vroom's expectancy theory is an example of this in that it takes into account the reasoning behind an individual's behaviour (Vroom, 1964). This theory is usually shown as an equation and proposes that there are three main requirements for motivation: expectancy, instrumentality and valence. The theory suggests that a person will be motivated to the degree that he or she believes that a given effort will lead to an acceptable performance (expectancy), that this performance will be rewarded (instrumentality) and that the reward will be one that is valued (valence).

All three factors must be present in order for motivation to occur and if an individual doesn't have faith in one aspect of the formula, motivation is likely to be much lower. For example, a student is confident that by carrying out focussed practice on a given task they expect to improve their skill sufficiently to pass an upcoming exam. Achieving a good outcome in the exam is important to them so they are motivated to put in the practice. However, what happens if they don't value the outcome? If they are not bothered whether they pass the exam or not? In this case the 'valence' part of the equation is not equivalent to the other two aspects and motivation is likely to be low. The same could happen if they valued the outcome but didn't believe that practice would make any difference.

Figure 4.2 Expectancy theory

An associated theory is that of goal setting, proposed by Latham and Locke (1991). This suggests that setting specific and measurable goals has a positive influence on motivation in that it provides a challenge which leads to enhanced performance. An important finding in this research was that for goals to be effective they also need to be challenging and that we are much more likely to be motivated by specific goals than we are by the 'do your best' type. More detail on how to use goals effectively in motivation is provided later in the chapter.

Humanist theories

Motivation is often referred to as a 'drive' which provides the force behind a particular action and this belief has led to ideas that motivation is in itself a form of drive reduction, in that it provides the impetus required for us to ensure our needs are met and that our minds and bodies return to a balanced state. This is similar to the notion of homeostasis – the way in which the body actively tries to maintain a certain equilibrium. When we are hungry, thirsty or cold we will be driven to actions which reduce these desires. A well-known theory of motivation, which is based on this principle, is Maslow's Hierarchy (1943) in which needs are presented in order of *prepotency* suggesting that we must work to satisfy *lower* needs before we are driven to meet those further up the hierarchy. Some examples are shown in Figure 4.3.

Figure 4.3 Adaption of Maslow's Hierarchy of Needs

Although a well-known and popular model of motivation there are some aspects of Maslow's hierarchy which may raise questions. For example, what do you understand by the term self-actualisation? Does the drive to self-actualise remain stable at different points in our lives? Might there be some individuals for whom 'self-actualisation', in whatever form it takes, is more important than more functional needs such as food or safety? The image of the driven, starving artist springs to mind here.

Maslow presents the notion of self-actualisation as a sort of innate drive to be the person we were meant to be: 'the desire to become more and more of what one is, to become everything that one is capable of becoming' (Maslow, 1943, p382), but how many people really know what (or who) that is? In order to become 'self-actualised' in Maslow's terms, we would also need to have very high levels of self-awareness and knowledge, otherwise we will never know when we have reached the peak of the triangle. More recent research (Krems et al., 2017) explored the notion of self-actualisation by gathering individual perceptions of the term to analyse whether this was a drive *above* and *divorced from* other biological or social needs. The researchers found that people often link self-actualisation to seeking status in life and this varies, often predictably, in accordance with what stage of life the individual is at. As a result, different drives would be more prominent at different points for everyone. In a teaching context this may be easier for a teacher to judge in phases of education which are organised by age, such as primary and secondary. In these cases, it can more easily be assumed that a particular cohort would be more or less at the same stage in life. In post compulsory education however, the picture is a little more complex and in a single cohort of students a teacher could be working with young adults, parents of teenage children, middle-aged 'career-changers' and people who have retired.

Another humanist idea linked to motivation is the importance of believing that we can achieve. According to Schunk (1984), people do not try hard at tasks if they feel they will fail. In contrast if we believe we can do something we are more likely to try harder. Bandura (1986) referred to this as *self-efficacy* and suggested that when *self-efficacy* was high, students would perform better. This idea is further supported by Dweck's work related to mindset (outlined in Chapter 2), suggesting that those students who believed they had *fixed* abilities were less likely to apply the necessary effort to a task than those who believed that they had *untapped potential*. The latter group, being more focussed on the developmental aspects of achievement, recognised that they may not be able to do a particular thing 'yet' and were therefore more likely to apply the necessary effort required to improve skills and knowledge (Dweck, 2008).

PAUSE POINT

Which of these theories might you be able to apply in your classroom? What practical strategies could you put in place to enhance learners' motivation?

CASE STUDY

Devi's journal

It has been two weeks of trying to implement the carrot and stick scheme and I am beginning to question my choices. I did exactly what my mentor advised, the idea is simple, I made it very clear to the students and I even reinforced it every lesson by providing opportunities for everyone to

(Continued)

(Continued)

earn points. I have definitely been consistent in my approach and I am certain the students know what is expected of them ... but it seems that they just don't care! I hate to admit it but this is really beginning to get to me ... I am not sure I can do this.

Even after observing other teachers in action I don't seem to have a clear answer on what works. Some teachers seem to use approaches based on sanctions and rewards, some used lots of questions, some, lots of activities. In fact, when I think about it, it seems that almost any approach can work ... It just doesn't seem to work for me!

I am beginning to despair. This is really having an impact on my own motivation. If I am honest I am not used to struggling with things ... maybe teaching just isn't for me? And I have to confess I am a little frustrated with my mentor. Why can't my mentor just tell me what to do? All I want is a technique or procedure to follow but I keep getting told to observe others, reflect on my actions and get curious about things ... really that isn't helpful at all!

Curiosity and motivation

Curiosity might be described as a cognitive process in that it is something which drives us to think about or explore a topic. In turn, curiosity leads to certain behaviours such as carrying out research or discussing ideas with others. When we become curious about something we are more likely to find opportunities to interact with it. In this sense curiosity itself provides a motivational drive; we become curious about something, we explore it, and the more curious we become the more motivated we will be to learn more. In a learning context this is an important idea and according to Silvia curiosity provides the intrinsic motivation required for effective learning: *by motivating people to learn for its own sake, interest ensures that people will develop a broad set of knowledge, skills, and experience* (Silvia, 2008, p57). But how do we do this? What is it that makes something interesting to a particular person or makes them curious to know more? If we only knew the answer to that question, motivating others would be very simple.

Inevitably, what people find interesting varies from one person to the next. We all have different likes and dislikes and by the time we become adults we have spent a lot of time cultivating these. We also see things differently depending on individual interpretations, therefore our perception of a given event is also likely to differ. Mezirow's work on frames of reference, outlining how individuals understand or *frame* their experiences highlights this lucidly and, according to Mezirow (1997), our frames of reference can also be changed or *transformed* if we take the time to think about and analyse them. In a sense, when we do this we are reframing our thoughts about particular experiences and in doing so are able to achieve a different perspective which, in turn, may lead to different behaviours. In Devi's case this process is beginning to take shape as she thinks about her lack of success in motivating her learners. While she acknowledges frustration at not having a particular formula to guide her, willingness to follow her mentor's advice about reflection and curiosity may be the first step to successful change.

What strategies could you use to encourage curiosity in your learners?

Figure 4.4 Curiouser and curiouser

Cultivating curiosity is a useful habit to develop. Being curious allows us to take an active rather than a passive role in learning and often makes us open to new ideas which in turn helps us to generate a 'deep' rather than 'surface' approach to our learning. In deep learning we are required to use higher-level skills such as analysis and synthesis, which in turn helps to deepen our understanding of a topic. In contrast, learning something at a surface level is when we might simply memorise (and soon forget) information for a particular purpose like an interview or an exam (Marton and Säljö, 1984). If you are not a naturally curious person, developing curiosity might take some practice and there are a few suggestions to try in Figure 4.5.

CASE STUDY

Devi's journal

I am really trying hard to cultivate my curiosity and I have actually been enjoying talking to others about teaching ... but I still crave having a step-by-step approach to follow! Strangely though, a sense of understanding is beginning to develop and, much as I hate to admit it, I am not sure I would have got to this point if I had simply followed a procedure. After reflecting on my observations and talking to some colleagues, I am beginning to believe that those teachers who are most successful in motivating learners are the ones who get to know them and try to adapt their teaching style to individuals and groups, rather than to particular topics. It seems obvious now I think about it! This is definitely something I can do, and I can even work with each individual student on finding goals that are specific and relevant for them. It feels like such a relief that I am beginning to get excited about teaching again.

Figure 4.5 Getting curious

Motivating through goals and targets

The significance of effective personal goal setting in raising motivation and achievement has been under-estimated; this could be because as teachers we don't make this a priority, or maybe it's because we're not very good at it? Yet, setting specific and challenging goals has been linked to improved performance and motivation. In Latham and Locke's study (1991), findings demonstrated that work performance was consistently improved when challenging goals were set for individuals and concluded that, provided adequate ability and commitment to the goal were present, the harder the goal, the higher the performance. This finding was attributed to the fact that people normally adjust their level of effort to the complexity of the task they are undertaking and therefore make more effort for difficult goals.

This seems like a very logical conclusion, so how can we translate this in relation to teaching and learning? What is it that makes a goal worth pursuing as opposed to something we simply write on an action plan and probably never refer to again?

For a goal to mean anything, it must be owned by the individual, rather than imposed upon them, and as simple as this concept should be to implement, there are often barriers in relation to goal ownership as well as to establishing meaningful goals. Learners are quite adept at telling us what we want to hear and may well produce goals that they think reflect this, rather than goals that may impact on the outcomes they actually want. Even if a learner does know what they want, they may not be able to articulate this and the real goal can get lost in the process.

One strategy for overcoming this is to place goal setting within a mentoring context, which means that it needs to be done on a one-to-one basis within a supportive framework. This doesn't necessarily mean that teachers have to work extra hours to achieve this, as opportunities can be built into classes whereby groups are kept actively employed in task-based learning so that teachers can allocate time to individual learners. Alternatively, the process can be supported by additional staff whose roles support teaching and learning activities.

Motivating yourself

Motivation is an important part of everyday life and impacts on our ability to achieve things. In teaching and learning it is generally assumed that the task of teaching and the effectiveness of learning are intrinsically connected to motivation, so teachers are well aware of their responsibilities in relation to motivating learners. However, what we often forget about is our own motivation. Motivated teachers, just like motivated learners, are key ingredients in positive learning environments. They are much more likely to try out new strategies, get excited by their work and infect others with their enthusiasm.

Vicious and virtuous circles in motivation

In the case of Devi, it was clear to see that her limited success in relation to motivating her group was also having a significant impact on her own learning. She was beginning to get frustrated with her lack of progress and with the absence of answers to her questions. These things had planted seeds of negativity which impacted on her beliefs about her own abilities and had the potential to turn into a vicious cycle. This, in turn, could provide further fuel for the initial damaging thoughts.

In most cases, negative or vicious cycles begin with irrational beliefs, ideas or expectations. These translate into destructive emotional states such as anger, anxiety and guilt. When we are over-whelmed by negative feelings it is difficult to engage with activities and, as a result, we are unlikely to do our best work. Subsequently, we experience more negativity and the cycle continues.

In Devi's case, she was able to stop the vicious cycle by expanding her curiosity and generating an interest in discussing ideas with her colleagues. This allowed her to regain her enthusiasm for teaching. In this way, Devi had begun a virtuous cycle which would more likely lead to favourable results and further reinforce her belief that she was able to find a solution to the current issue. Like Devi, we all have the potential to get ourselves into vicious thought cycles and spotting these is very useful in the process of turning negative situations into positive ones.

ACTIVITY 4.1

List the things which may start your own vicious cycle. For each thing on the list, think about an alternative strategy which could turn your vicious cycle into a virtuous one.

Figure 4.6 Vicious cycle

Vicious cycles have the potential to become self-fulfilling prophecies (Merton, 1968), which simply means that our beliefs or expectations influence how we behave and lead to the belief becoming true. Merton described this as: *A false definition of the situation evoking a new behaviour which makes the originally false conception come true* (1968, p477). For example, we may generate the belief that we are 'not good enough' to apply for a promotion at work. If that belief is fuelled by continuous thoughts of 'not good enough', what are we likely to do when an opportunity for promotion presents itself? Most of us would not apply for the job and as a result the belief that we are not good enough will have come true.

Turning vicious cycles into virtuous ones initially requires corrective thinking which aims to highlight any irrational thoughts or beliefs so that these can be reframed in more rational ways. This may be done by talking through concerns with others, trying to change negative self-talk into more neutral or positive statements and resetting unhelpful mental images with more realistic ones.

Practising active motivation

We tend to assume that motivation is a natural state or attribute, perhaps something that some people have in abundance and others do not, but is this really the case, or is it something we can apply ourselves to in much the same way as we would develop any other skill?

A strategy for building motivation is to actively practise it. We can do this by applying new ideas to our work or our personal goals, creating things, accepting mistakes as part of a process and seeing problems as potential challenges. If this is the case, one of the most important things we can do is to make it easy to start doing whatever it is we want to do. In Devi's case she simply observed other teachers and then found the opportunity to discuss her ideas. This didn't require any special skill or a huge investment of time. It was easy and allowed her to see potential solutions to her own challenges.

It may also be useful to schedule motivation, or activities we find motivating, in the same way as we may schedule other parts of our day. This is common practice for many well-known creators, for example, novelist Haruki Murakami writes ten pages a day, then runs ten kilometres before undertaking the rest of the day's activities (Marukami, 2014). Maya Angelou (poet and writer) used to rent a local hotel room to write. She would arrive early in the morning, write until early afternoon, then go home to do some editing. She never slept at the hotel (Writers Write, online). While we all have to undertake certain work tasks that do not necessarily motivate us, there are likely to be other things which do, so each of us has the opportunity to schedule motivating activities which will help to maintain our motivation equilibrium.

Chapter summary

In this chapter we have explored traditional theories of motivation and considered their application to the classroom. We have also considered how teachers may motivate individual students through the use of specific goals. While some of the theories may seem directly applicable to your teaching, the usefulness of others may not be quite as apparent. What is important is that you approach all theory with an open mind, think about it, question it and try to adapt it in ways which will work for you. Perhaps the most important thing to take from this chapter is to think about how you maintain your own motivation, as this is the key to your continued development as a professional teacher.

MENTOR MOMENT

In this section we have included starter points for discussions with mentors to provide an opportunity for you to talk through the chapter content. The aim of the questions is to encourage you to interrogate your understanding of the concepts presented and consider ways in which these might influence your teaching.

- What do motivated students 'look like'?
- Which of the theories presented link to your vision of motivation?
- What strategies could you try to generate student motivation?
- How will you keep yourself motivated?

——— Suggested further reading ———————————————————————

Dweck, **CS** (2017) *Mindset: Changing the Way You Think to Fulfil Your Potential*. New York: Ballantine.

Locke, **EA and Latham**, **GP** (2013) *New Developments in Goal Setting and Task Performance*. Abingdon: Routledge.

——— References ———————————————————————————————

Bandura, **A** (1986) The explanatory and predictive scope of self-efficacy theory. *Journal of Clinical and Social Psychology*, 4 (3): 359–73.

Dweck, **CS** (2008) *Mindset: The New Psychology of Success*. New York: Ballantine.

Krems, **AJ**, **Kenrick**, **DT and Neel**, **R** (2017) Individual perceptions of self-actualization: what functional motives are linked to fulfilling one's full potential? *Personality and Social Psychology Bulletin*, 43 (9): 1337–52 **doi: 10.1177/0146167217713191**

Latham, **GP and Locke**, **EA** (1991) Self-regulation through goal setting. *Organizational Behavior and Human Decision Processes*, 50 (2): 212–47 **http://dx.doi.org/10.1016/0749-5978(91)90021-K**

Marton, **F and Säljö**, **R** (1984) Approaches to learning, in Marton, F, Hounsell, D and Entwistle, N (eds) *The Experience of Learning*. Edinburgh: Scottish Academic Press.

Marukami, **H** (2014) *Men without Women*. London: Vintage.

Maslow, **AH** (1943) A theory of human motivation, in Merton, RK (ed) (1968) *Social Theory and Social Structure*. New York: Free Press.

Merton, **RK** (1968) *Social Theory and Social Structure*. New York: Free Press.

Mezirow, **J** (1997) *Transformative Dimensions of Adult Learning*. San Francisco, CA: Jossey-Bass.

Schunk, **DH** (1984) Enhancing self-efficacy and achievement through rewards and goals: motivational and informational effects. *Journal of Educational Research*, 78 (1): 29–34.

Silvia, **PJ** (2008) Interest: the curious emotion. *Current Directions in Psychological Science*, 17 (1): 57–60.

Vroom, **VH** (1964) *Work and Motivation*. San Francisco, CA: Jossey-Bass.

Writers Write Maya Angelou's writing process. Available at **https://writerswrite.co.za/maya-angelous-writing-process/** (Accessed 13 January 2019).

5

DEVELOPING LEARNERS' THINKING

In this chapter we will explore:

- what is meant by constructivism;
- the connection between cognitivism and constructivism;
- some of the theorists connected with constructivism;
- the principles of constructivist learning;
- how these principles are applied in the classroom.

Introduction

Constructivism and constructivist teaching are things which many teachers, new and experienced, find very difficult to implement in the classroom. Although outwardly a very simple process, resting as it does on the principle of encouraging students to take more responsibility for their own learning, constructivism can represent a very challenging course of action for teachers to incorporate into their professional practice. In this chapter we will explore the nature of this challenge, how it can be met and how, by doing so, constructivism can enable teachers to make their classroom a more efficient and effective place for learning and teaching. Having said all that, constructivist teaching is not something to be embarked upon lightly; it doesn't work in every situation and it doesn't work for every student. As ever, there are a number of variables which must be taken into account when considering constructivist teaching: the nature of the students, the level of learning, the subject matter, the ethos of the classroom itself, but probably the most important considerations are the attitude and confidence level of the teacher. In this chapter we meet Pat, a young teacher eager to experiment with new methods to improve learning.

Figure 5.1 Pat's story

> ## CASE STUDY
>
> ### Pat's journal
>
> *Okay, I'm knee-deep in preparations for the new term and it's really exciting. I've been given the chance to teach the HND and A level groups this year and I'm quite determined to make it as interesting as possible. I remember only too well how bored I was when I took my A levels. It wasn't the subjects themselves – I was really interested in them – it was just the way that they were taught. Lecture after lecture, presentation after presentation, just taking notes and writing things down. Ugh!! I'm not going to inflict that on my students! Just got to figure out how I can make learning more interesting so that they understand the subject rather than just being able to repeat facts.*

Constructivist learning

That's quite a task that Pat has set out to achieve. Making learning interesting, finding new ways of learning and making sure that students understand the subject. Students construct their understanding of the subjects in different ways. Although all learning starts with sensory processing – the taking in of information through the senses by reading, listening, watching or doing something – much of what is experienced in this way goes into short-term memory and is forgotten fairly quickly. Eysenck and Keane (2005, p1) argue that learning *is concerned with the internal processes involved in making sense of the environment and deciding what action might be appropriate.* The sensory and short-term memory processing systems can only analyse a situation. However, these systems work in conjunction with long-term memory to recall and retrieve information previously stored in the long-term memory to either deal with the situation (as Eysenck and Keane propose) or add information into an existing schema for future reference as Piaget (1936) suggests. Both these processes require students to actively engage and take part in (either knowingly or unknowingly) a learning process and, through participation, Hartley (1998, p11) indicates that *instead of acquiring habits, learners acquire plans and strategies* to use knowledge and make connections between different elements, facts, concepts and ideas.

> ## CASE STUDY
>
> ### Pat's journal
>
> *Right, I seem to be giving them lots of things to do and think about but they don't seem to be making connections between things or thinking for themselves; they seem to be content with just learning facts. I'm doing all the work at the moment and it feels as though I'm spoon-feeding them to get them to make sense of things – this isn't what I wanted – something needs to change, but what?*

What both Pat and the students are experiencing is trouble in making the move from cognitivism (see Chapter 3) to constructivism. In cognitivist teaching it is the teacher who adopts responsibility for learning, chunking up information or 'knowledge' into bite-size pieces and presenting it to students in ways which help them assimilate or 'learn' it. Admittedly, for constructivist teaching to succeed there is a need for there to be a firm foundation of knowledge on which to build, but this early in the academic year Pat may still need to ensure that students have this secure foundation of underpinning knowledge and may need to be teaching cognitively. However, Pat is right in saying that things need to change in order to move the students from simply accepting prescribed information to making use of it as a tool for critical thinking (Knight, 2015) as discussed in Chapter 1. The changes that Pat recognises need to be made are in two areas.

1. The realignment of the roles and responsibilities for acquiring learning.

2. What learning is and how learning can be achieved.

The theories underpinning constructivism

Vygotsky (1978), building on the work of Piaget, recognises three key factors in learning.

1. The recognition of Zones of Proximal Development (ZPD).

2. The role of a More Knowledgeable Other (MKO).

3. The role of Social Interaction in learning.

From the journal entry it is clear that Pat recognises that there is a gap between what the students are able to do and what they need to be able to do – what Vygotsky would describe as the Zone of Proximal Development (ZPD). A ZPD can exist in any of the domains of learning (see Chapter 3) and occurs when the existing physical, mental/attitudinal skills or knowledge are insufficient for the group or individual to progress to the next stage of learning. With guidance and encouragement from someone with the appropriate knowledge or skills – the More Knowledgeable Other (MKO) identified by Vygotsky – the skills/knowledge needed by students to successfully navigate the ZPD can be developed. However, the development of the required skills/knowledge will need to be supported by the MKO through a process described by Bruner (1960) as scaffolding. For Bruner (1978, p19), scaffolding consists of the *steps taken to reduce the degrees of freedom in carrying out ... [the] ... task so that ... [the student] ... can concentrate on the* skills/knowledge they are in the process of acquiring. In the construction of a new building, scaffolding limits and defines the shape of the building itself while at the same time providing a safe space in which the builders can construct the building. In education, the scaffold is derived from a constructive interaction between the MKO and the student with the objective of assisting the student to achieve a specific outcome. Initially formed from the primary information given to the students by the MKO (often using cognitive teaching methods) the scaffolding temporarily limits the students' knowledge but focusses their attention on the subject matter and provides a secure framework within which individual students can begin to construct or develop schema.

Figure 5.2 ZPD

ACTIVITY 5.1

Think about Pat's situation and jot down your thoughts about the following questions.

- What is the nature of the ZPD that Pat's students have to cross?
- Who are the MKOs those students may be able to access to acquire the skills/knowledge necessary to move across the ZPD?
- What can Pat do to build the scaffold to help students learn?

At the moment Pat recognises that a ZPD exists between what the students are able to do (recognising and absorbing information – learning cognitively) and what they need to be able to do (make connections between pieces of information and critically assess their relative importance – constructing new knowledge). In essence, Pat's students appear to be lacking the higher-level thinking skills of evaluation, analysis and synthesis identified by Bloom et al. (1956). With guidance and encouragement from Pat acting as an MKO these skills can be developed but they will need to be carefully scaffolded by creative teaching methods which both support and challenge the students in order to enable them to cultivate these skills. Pat, however, is not the only potential MKO available to the students. As noted in Chapter 3 students learn at different paces and construct their understanding of new knowledge in diverse ways. Vygotsky argued that during interaction with peers who have a more advanced or different way of understanding the subject, a student could adopt the role of an MKO, acting as a critical friend to challenge and extend existing schema for other students.

Bruner's (1978) theories on learning, although separated in temporal terms from those of Vygotsky who developed his theories in Stalinist Russia in the 1920s (but whose work only became available in the West in the 1970s), are similar to them in some respects. While both saw the importance of learners interacting with and making meaning of subject matter in their own way, their view of the role of the teacher as part of this process was different. Rather than being led by the teacher as an MKO modelling the processes of organising and categorising information for students as suggested by Vygotsky, Bruner (1978) argued that students should actively discover links between pieces of information for themselves through a process he described as discovery learning. For both theorists, the need for individuals to create links between items of information was a critical element in the learning process, but for Bruner the most important outcome was for the individual to develop the ability to find answers for themselves by developing their problem-solving processes and procedures.

One point of agreement between Bruner and Vygotsky was, however, that learning could be promoted by individuals participating in social interaction. By taking part in argument or discussion with peers or MKOs, the individual is actively participating in the processes of meaning-making (making sense of things) and constructing new knowledge by adding to their existing understanding. Alternative ways of presenting or explaining information or situations given by MKOs can both challenge their existing thinking and enable them to grasp concepts and ideas in ways which are unique to them. Through social interaction with MKOs students can gain experience in constructing new systems of meaning (the ways in which they individually interpret and understand the subject).

Teaching and learning in a constructivist manner is challenging for both students and teachers as it requires both to change their relationship with the learning process. The change of role for the teacher from that of a pedagogue who controls the learning process, determining both the information given and the way in which it is received, to that of a guide and mentor, challenging students to develop their own understanding, is a difficult one. Learning to 'let go', to relinquish control of a classroom situation while simultaneously retaining responsibility for student learning, is definitely not an easy task for any teacher. Equally, the need for students to change their relationships to learning is not easy. Most students have been conditioned to be passive recipients of information and identify this process as 'learning'. In constructivism the student has to grasp the idea that learning is an individual process and requires their active participation in establishing relationships between existing facts or pieces of knowledge in order to construct new knowledge. This process of constructing knowledge is unique to the individual; no two individuals can ever have had exactly the same learning experiences, and each individual builds on, and links together, their previous experiences and understandings with new knowledge.

Constructivism in a nutshell

- Constructivism is about the development of new knowledge by the individual.

- Learning is an individual process.

- There is a need for the student to be guided across the unknown, but the process of meaning-making and constructing new knowledge by linking new understanding with existing knowledge is an individual one.

- Students may need to develop new skills to help them in problem-solving.

- The roles of the teacher and student change from that of the teacher controlling the learning process with the student as passive recipient of knowledge to that of mentor/guide and student relationship with both working collaboratively to enable the student to construct new knowledge and understanding.

- Learning is a social activity involving interaction with others, both peers and MKOs.

CASE STUDY

Pat's journal

Right, enough spoon-feeding! The students have got all the foundation material and readings, etc. for this unit now and I have to make them begin to think for themselves. This unit has a written assignment and I would normally give them a lot of guidance in what is wanted; I think this time they need to work it out for themselves. After all they are going to have to do this for themselves when they get to university or out into the workplace – they might as well find out how to do it now!

Pat's journal

Oh heck!! It's a disaster!! The assignments were dreadful – they showed no signs of joined-up thinking at all; all they were doing was trying to regurgitate facts that I have given them. I gave them loads of time to work on their own, but it seems that they haven't learned anything – most of them haven't made any connections and if any of them have made a connection of any sort it's been cut and pasted from something they have read on the internet – they just can't do this. What am I doing wrong? Help!!!!!!

ACTIVITY 5.2

Having looked at Pat's journal entries, note down your thoughts about the following questions.

- What do you think of the problems?
- How do you think that they could be overcome by using constructivist teaching and learning?

Well, from the first entry it looks as though Pat has decided to 'let go', but as you see from the following entry just 'letting go' isn't enough. 'Letting go' does not imply that the teacher can abdicate their responsibility for the learning process – constructivism is not simply a matter of leaving students the time and space to learn for themselves. Constructivist teaching and learning needs to be carefully planned and monitored in order to be effective.

Going back over the journal entries it would seem that Pat has only partially identified his students' ZPD. Pat can see that they are 'regurgitating facts' rather than constructing knowledge, making connections and critiquing different elements. The foundation of 'knowledge' which Pat has given to his students provides a platform for their future learning, but learning is an active process as well as individual activity and consists not only of constructing meaning but also building systems of meaning. From the journal entries Pat doesn't appear to recognise the necessity of teaching the students the skills (in this case the higher-level thinking skills) needed to construct Bruner's systems of meaning.

One of the things that Pat needs to consider is the students' motivation, what Knowles et al. (2015) describe as their readiness to learn. Pat could have promoted their readiness, or motivation to participate in learning, by introducing what Ausubel (1960) describes as advance or forward organisers – a three-phase system which provides a firm scaffold within which students can safely learn new material or integrate new ideas into existing schemas. In phase one, the teacher builds the foundations of the scaffold by giving a clear explanation of the aims of the lesson, what students will be expected to learn, what it is that they will be doing to learn and why. Explaining the aims and objectives in language that students understand, and making connections with previous lessons, enables the students to understand the context of the new learning and prepare their existing schemas to receive the new information and/or make connections with existing knowledge. Preparing the students in this way helps to motivate the students to learn as they have been provided with a 'route map' showing both the destination and the route (or process) for learning. The second phase involves the logical presentation of the subject matter to the students. Using tasks and activities designed to meet the learning objectives the teacher designs and builds the scaffold while ensuring that the students are actively engaged constructing new knowledge within a bespoke framework. The final phase is designed to enable students to expand or strengthen their unique systems of meaning (their individual interpretation and understanding of the new learning). In this phase the student is actively encouraged by the teacher to adopt a critical approach to the new knowledge by thinking about the contradictions or connections with previous learning. In this way the teacher facilitates students to make meaning and build their knowledge and understanding of the subject within the safe space provided by the scaffold.

Introducing advance organisers into teaching can be seen as a foundation for putting into practice the nine principles of constructivist learning suggested by Hein (1991).

1. Learning is an active process in which the learner constructs meaning from sensory input.

2. Learning involves both the construction of meaning and building of systems of meaning – students learn how they learn as they develop their individual systems of meaning.

3. Constructing meaning is an individual mental activity.

4. The use of language is important as students need to understand what it is they are expected to learn to be able to do and to appropriate new vocabulary into their schema.

5. Learning is a social activity associated with a connection with other people.

6. The context of learning is important. Learning is contextual: we do not learn isolated facts and theories in some abstract ethereal land of the mind separate from the rest of our lives; we learn in relationship to what else we know.

7. Previous knowledge is necessary as it forms a basis for the formation of new knowledge.

8. Learning takes time – creating and establishing systems of meaning is a gradual process.

9. Learners need to be motivated in order to learn – people need to know why they are doing something and what it is they are supposed to achieve.

PAUSE POINT

Think about your own learning and teaching and decide which of the nine principles of constructivist learning you are using. What is the impact of these principles being used/not used on the process of learning for your students?

Developing a constructivist classroom

Learning in partnership

One of the things that worries teachers about using constructivist teaching methods is that they feel their influence over the students' learning may be diminished. However, constructivist learning is built on a partnership between the student and teacher with the teacher acting as a director of studies. In this role the teacher retains responsibility for learning by empowering students to take responsibility for their learning through coaching, modelling and scaffolding the learning process. By designing activities in which students can participate the teacher is helping them to construct new knowledge and systems of meaning. A further reservation that may be expressed by teachers is that constructivist classrooms can appear to outsiders to be noisy and lacking in direction. Most teachers are used to classrooms in which students are studying diligently, quietly absorbing prescribed knowledge through reading, writing or researching. Constructivist classrooms are, however, based on different principles; learning is an active, collaborative and social activity which involves discussion and structured, interactive group work to facilitate students in the creation of unique understandings and systems of meaning, activities which generally generate a level of noise.

Introducing spiral curricula

Creating knowledge and developing systems of meaning are evolutionary learning processes. One of the things Pat might consider in promoting these processes is the introduction of a spiral curriculum (Bruner, 1960). By revisiting a topic or subject several times over a period of time and increasing the complexity of the subject each time, difficult or complex information is put into context and the student is able to establish the relationship between new and previous learning. Revisiting the subject in this way not only gives the teacher the opportunity to assess current learning before adding new information, it provides a safe intellectual environment in which students can reflect on their learning and take risks when expressing opinions or discussing potential knowledge or connections. Revisiting the subject, however, does not imply that the same learning methods should be used each time. Once the basic information has been given the teacher's role becomes that of developing the scaffold for learning.

Building scaffolds for learning

The scaffold for learning can be designed by the teacher through the use of interactive activities carefully constructed to meet the learning objectives. In constructivism the teacher is often building the lessons around a 'big idea' or abstract concept which the students need to understand in order to progress. Ideally, the activities needed to help them to grasp these new ideas involve students in some form of activity. This does not, however, imply that the activity is a physical one; more often than not the students' activity is intellectual and social. Interaction with others, either peers or the MKO, motivates students by encouraging them to put forward or discuss ideas. Activities such as case studies, small group projects, demonstrations followed by discussion, carousel activities, brainstorming, buzz sessions, collaborative concept mapping, etc., etc., etc., are activities which will help students develop their understanding of new information. In these activities preconceptions may be challenged, existing schema developed or altered, and new knowledge constructed both jointly and severally by students.

Developing thinking skills

One of the problems Pat experienced was that the students did not possess the high-level thinking skills which are needed for constructivist learning. While the activities just mentioned may be primarily aimed at enabling students to construct a new knowledge, activities can at the same time be used to develop thinking skills. Activities such as ideas speed dating, where students present their insights about a topic several times over a period to a different peer or peers and receive feedback, can help them develop the skills of analysis, evaluation and synthesis. Encouraging students to use mind maps or to produce mind maps in groups can help students to develop and see connections between ideas, concepts and facts. A simple idea, such as giving students different coloured pens or crayons when they are creating group mind maps, can help students to see not only their own contribution to the mind map but also let them see how their personal views and understanding are growing and changing.

Activity with a purpose

When using these activities it is essential that the students understand that the activities have a purpose, and understand what that purpose is. Without this understanding students will remember the activity but not how it helped them to meet the learning objective and if the activity takes too long or is lacking in focus it may not achieve its objectives. One method I favour for encouraging students to remain 'on task' when undertaking constructivist activities is to implement the ten-minute rule. No activity lasts for more than ten minutes and it is followed by a related activity which can either be aimed at deepening students' understanding or encouraging them to explore the subject further. A couple of minutes may be added to the activities in order to obtain students' feedback on what they have learned from participating in the activity; their thoughts can be noted down on the board either by a scribe appointed by the group or by the teacher and are referred back to by the teacher at the end of the next activity. By showing the connections between the activities, the teacher is demonstrating not only that they are actively engaged with the students, but they are also modelling the different ways in which systems of meaning can be developed while still retaining control of the learning process.

The teacher's role in a constructivist classroom is a critical one. Not only are they the director of studies choosing and setting appropriate activities, they are also a guide and mentor for the students. By seeking feedback from students from their activities the teacher is demonstrating not only that they value the students' inputs and points of view, but they are also providing an opportunity for peers acting as MKOs to challenge students' suppositions. By asking probing questions or posing contradictory ideas or concepts as part of the post-activity discussions with students the teacher is able to extend or advance their higher-level thinking processes.

CASE STUDY

Pat's journal

Well we're getting there. Changing the activities in the classroom and making it more interactive rather than taking the lead all the time has certainly helped students in making connections between things. Encouraging them to think for themselves, letting them make mistakes and find the corrections, letting other students critique peer opinions in a collaborative and co-operative atmosphere has certainly meant that they are taking more responsibility for their own learning. We have a little way to go yet but they are almost ready to start work on their individual projects - I never thought at the beginning of the year that I would get them to this stage! I won't pretend it's not been hard work or that we haven't gone down a few blind alleys (not many, just one or two when my planning was not quite as good as it might have been), but the students have increased in confidence and their academic skills as well as their knowledge are improving - most importantly, they enjoyed learning. Success!!!

As Pat noted in the journal entry, constructivist teaching is not an easy option. It means both students and teachers learning new skill sets and roles and accepting different responsibilities in terms of teaching and learning. It requires careful planning and the use of focussed activities, but most of all it requires a partnership approach to learning. Teachers and students both need to understand what is required and must be able to communicate with each other in a supportive and safe learning environment where challenge and criticism is seen as a constructive process enabling growth by both parties. It's not an easy option but it is one that is rewarding for both the teacher and the student.

Chapter summary

In this chapter we have looked at the meaning of constructivism, the differences between cognitivism and constructivism, and how cognitive teaching and learning can act as a foundation for constructivist learning. We have looked at the roles and responsibilities that need to be adopted in the constructivist classroom by both the teacher and students and the difficulties that may be encountered in changing traditional roles. The theory of constructivism has been investigated, and its main principles and how these can be introduced into a classroom setting discussed.

MENTOR MOMENT

Constructivist teaching is not something that suits every student or teacher. As with all things in teaching it takes time and practice. As we indicated at the beginning of this chapter it is something that can be of great benefit to students, preparing them for more than study by teaching them how to learn, and how they, as an individual, construct new knowledge and understanding. Think about the following questions and discuss them with your mentor.

- How appropriate is constructivist teaching for the students you teach?
- What steps could you take to make your teaching more constructivist?
- What do you think the benefits of constructivist teaching will be for you and your students?
- How do you think your students would react to being taught in this way?

Suggested further reading

Beck, C and Kosnik, C (2006) *Innovations in Teacher Education: A Social Constructivist Approach*. New York: State University of New York Press.

Stabile, C and Ershler, J (2015) *Constructivism Reconsidered in the Age of Social Media: New Directions for Teaching and Learning*. New York: Wiley.

References

Ausubel, DP (1960) The use of advance organizers in the learning and retention of meaningful verbal material. *Journal of Educational Psychology*, 51: 267–72.

Bloom, B, Englehart, MD, Furst, E, Hill, W and Krathwohl, D (1956) *Taxonomy of Educational Objectives: The Classification of Educational Goals. Handbook I: Cognitive Domain*. New York, Toronto: Longmans, Green.

Bruner, JS (1960) *The Process of Education*. Cambridge, MA: Harvard University Press.

Bruner, JS (1978) The role of dialogue in language acquisition, in Sinclair, A, Jarvelle, RJ and Levelt, WJM (eds) *The Child's Concept of Language*. New York: Springer-Verlag.

Eysenck, MW and Keane, MT (2005) *Cognitive Psychology: A Student Handbook*. Hove: Psychology Press Ltd.

Hartley, J (1998) *Learning and Studying: A Research Perspective*. London: Routledge.

Hein, GE (1991) 'Constructivist learning theory', The museum and the needs of people. CECA (International Committee of Museum Educators) Conference, Jerusalem. *Israel*, 15–22 October 1991 **www.exploratorium.edu/IFI/resources/constructivistlearning.html**

Knight, R (2015) Postgraduate student teachers' developing conceptions of the place of theory in learning to teach: 'more important to me now than when I started'. *Journal of Education for Teaching*, 41 (2): 145–60.

Knowles, MS, Holton, EF and Swanson, RA (2015) *The Adult Learner* (8th ed). Abingdon: Routledge.

Piaget, J (1936) *Origins of Intelligence in the Child*. London: Routledge and Kegan Paul.

Vygotsky, LS (1978) *Mind in Society: The Development of Higher Psychological Processes*. Cambridge, MA: Harvard University Press.

6

LEARNING WITH OTHERS

In this chapter we will explore:

- social learning theory;
- classroom collaboration;
- collegiality and teacher collaboration.

Introduction

Unless we choose to live in complete isolation, spending time with others is a part of daily life and this is no exception in the classroom. The days of tutor-led, didactic teaching are, in most learning environments, a thing of the past and the benefits of taking a more collaborative approach to learning are widely recognised in the world of education and beyond. Yet, there is often a misunderstanding of the word 'collaboration' and how this can most usefully be translated into a learning environment:

> In our school we all get along, we co-operate, discuss and share resources; we work side by side, help each other out, and support each other. We work together on committees, sports teams and special events. We're very collaborative ... aren't we?
>
> (Sharratt and Planche, 2016)

This quote certainly describes a collegiate environment but it is questionable whether 'getting along' and 'supporting each other' is the most purposeful form of collaboration. Indeed, in some cases this may just as easily lead to maintaining the current status quo and if we are to engage in purposeful collaboration it follows that collaboration must also include challenge.

Learning from others is a natural part of our developmental process and in this chapter we will learn the ways in which we learn both from and with other people. This will involve exploring the almost 'incidental' learning which takes place through social modelling and situated learning, as well as more directed forms of collaboration such as group work. We will also consider how teachers can collaborate in ways which will have a positive impact on teaching and learning.

In this chapter we are introduced to Milena, an experienced teacher who is finding managing her teaching alongside studying for her PGCE to be quite a challenge. As part of her studies Milena has been studying collaborative approaches to learning and this is something she wants to make more of in her lessons.

Figure 6.1 Milena's story

CASE STUDY

Milena's journal

On my PGCE we learned about social learning theory and how people learn from observing and imitating others. Apparently through some form of collaboration learning occurs at a deeper level ... presumably this means it is something I need to include in my lessons? I can model the behaviours I want in the class, I think I probably do that already as my students seem well aware of the importance of listening to me ... but how do I get them to work effectively together? The trouble is they have no discipline and I can see them running wild if I don't control every aspect of the class. If the last few years has taught me anything, it's that students are not naturally motivated ... and I need to keep them on task by carefully managing the classroom activities. I always prepare very structured lessons which helps but it also means that I spend a lot of time talking and the only input the students have is when I ask them questions. They have also become quite adept at working out what I want from them; they are good at giving the right answers but I am never sure how much they are really learning and wonder if I need to change my approach? I guess this means I might also have to lose a bit of control? That makes me nervous but I am also fascinated to see if this works!

Social learning theory

Social learning theory is based on the premise that interaction with others is a fundamental part of our development. Bandura (1986) suggests that as children we observe the people around us and based on these observations, learn particular behaviours. This form of social imitation is not dissimilar to the way that other species learn; for example, young animals quite naturally mimic the behaviours of the adults within their groups and through this process learn to fit in with the community. Likewise, children are quite adept at copying the behaviours they see, even if we don't want them to. Bandura used the term 'social modelling' to describe how we might learn from particular role models in our lives. Based on this theory it is easy to see how learners might adopt certain behaviours in the classroom by copying their peers, by replicating behaviours they have seen in other classroom settings or by copying their teachers. Most experienced teachers will be able to cite examples of where this can help to create a positive learning environment and might also be able to provide as many examples of where copying learned behaviours does not result in a positive outcome. We quite naturally learn positive and negative things through our observation and imitation of others so this is something all teachers need to be mindful of. Part of the job description for a teacher is to act as a role model for learners and, as such, be aware of the influence they have over behaviour in the classroom. This involves modelling prosocial behaviours such as respect for others, listening to points of view, turn-taking and so on but it also includes minimising behaviours which might be considered antisocial as opposed to prosocial, for example, talking over others, interrupting or swearing.

Milena is quite aware of this as she has managed to instil the message that it is important to listen in the classroom. Her students are behaving appropriately but she still doesn't believe that they are actually motivated about learning. So what's missing?

At a superficial level it appears that the teacher's main role in this is to manage the classroom environment to ensure that it remains prosocial rather than antisocial and a useful strategy for this is to model the behaviours that are expected from others. If the theory is adopted at this level it is likely to have some positive impact but it also suggests that we simply need to demonstrate and reinforce the behaviours we want others to reproduce and they will copy them, without taking into account their own intrinsic motivations or interpretations of a given situation. But do we simply copy others, or do we make choices about our behaviours based on how we are making sense of a given situation, or how we have learned to behave in similar situations in the past? Milena's students appear to have learned that their role is to listen in class and to give the right answers to questions. They may be learning some facts through this process but do they have the opportunity to interact with the new learning and to make sense of it for themselves?

While often described as a behaviourist theory which is dependent on reinforcement and repetition, social learning is also influenced by a number of internal factors such as satisfaction and sense of accomplishment. It is not simply a response to a given stimulus. In Bandura's view, reinforcement could be internal or external and, as a result, people do not simply model or imitate all the behaviours they observe. Instead, he suggested that there is a mediational process through which the observation of a behaviour and the response to it are reconciled. For example, if we are seeking the approval of another, we might exhibit the behaviours which get an external reinforcement such as a smile or a pat on the back. If these are things which will make us feel good (an internal process) it is likely that we might repeat these behaviours. However, if the reinforcements are not things we value, it is likely that the behaviours will not be repeated and in this way we are mediating our responses through a cognitive process which allows us to think about and judge what is of value to us. Therefore, social learning theory takes thought processes into account and acknowledges the importance they have in mediating our responses to particular situations.

The balance between control and freedom to learn

Milena is fearful that by relinquishing some of her control of classroom activity she will encourage chaos in the classroom and this means she won't be able to focus on her teaching, which appears to be structured around explaining and asking questions.

Explaining is an important part of the teacher's role and an essential part of the learning process but it is also something we can easily develop an over-reliance upon. Our explanations give students the benefit of our knowledge and experience, but is it possible that too much explaining can have a detrimental effect on learning? Teacher talk still appears to be quite dominant in classrooms and, according to Littleton et al. (2005), 70–90 per cent of classroom time is taken up with talking rather than discussion, and in records of classroom discussion Clinton et al. (2014) discovered that 89 percent of the talking that went on in classrooms was done by teachers.

It is easy to see why teachers use 'teacher talk' as a dominant strategy in classroom management and Milena is no exception in this. By ensuring she explains things clearly and manages learner activities, she has a close control on everything that happens and can feel confident that the specific learning objectives she has set out will be achieved. At one level this is sensible – the teacher is the person who has designed the lesson and as such is the one who has the overview of the intended learning and the steps needed to get to the desired point – but it could also be argued that this level of control can inhibit progress. What if the learners could move overall learning beyond the objectives designed by the teacher? What if the examples and ideas they share could provide a more palatable forum from which to construct understanding? Milena should also consider the covert messages she is giving to learners by closely controlling all classroom activity. Are these the actions of a teacher who believes her students are motivated and will behave appropriately, or do they represent a teacher who does not believe her students want to learn and expects them to behave badly?

In *Freedom to Learn*, Rogers (1969) discussed the difficulties associated with controlling classroom activities within formalised learning and suggested that learning should be an experiential process whereby the material presented would become more meaningful to learners. In this way learners would be provided with opportunities to confront problems and develop new skills to overcome them, becoming more independent and, as a result, learning how to learn. Rogers is often cited as the thinker at the forefront of teaching as facilitation rather than instruction suggesting that we cannot actually teach anyone directly, rather we provide the conditions in which they can learn (Rogers, 1969). Similar views are expressed by Kolb (1984) in his four-stage model of experiential learning (see Figure 6.2), whereby learning is said to occur through a process of experience, reflection, creating understanding and considering solutions or changes.

Figure 6.2 Adapted from Kolb's experiential learning cycle

In contrast, Hattie suggests that *direct instruction* is a top teaching strategy, whereas *giving students control over their learning* was considered to have little or no impact (Hattie online) and, according to Ashman (2018), *explicit instruction* is a key part of effective teaching and learning.

Classroom collaboration

According to Hattie and Zierer (2018), successful collaboration in the classroom can have a substantial impact on learning and is something which both teachers and learners can benefit from. But, to make this strategy beneficial we do need an understanding of the process of collaboration and, more specifically, the different roles that teachers and learners play in this.

A general definition of collaborative learning would be any form of active learning that involves two or more students working together on something, which means that there are a wide range of activities which could be encompassed under this heading. The main difference between this and other teaching methods is that learning is dependent on learners' exploration and application of information as opposed to a teacher's presentation of it. Collaboration can take a variety of forms.

- *Collaborative learning*, where learners work alongside each other towards a common goal, for example working out a response to a particular question. The aim is for them to self-manage this process and to learn to work together on a task.

- *Co-operative learning*, which is usually a structured activity with inherent interdependence, like putting together a theatrical performance whereby each learner would have a specific role and level of accountability but each was dependent on others for the overall success.

- *Competition*, whereby teams are created and learners must work in co-operative ways to ensure the team's success.

Each of these approaches has individual benefits and can be employed to develop learners' interpersonal skills as well as to provide opportunities for them to interact with new information.

The benefits of learning in peer groups have been recognised for some time as an effective form of pedagogy believed to promote learning and higher-level thinking. These types of activities also help to encourage the development of prosocial behaviours (Gillies et al., 2008) and can make us more effective in achieving our goals. Research into *social synchrony* (Miles et al., 2010; Wheatley et al., 2012) suggests that when we work with others towards a shared goal the energy produced is tangible and creates a cognitive, affective and behavioural connection which allows us to share thoughts and feelings successfully. This can be witnessed in symbols related to interpersonal rapport, such as imitation of body language or physical energy, but also has a practical value in reducing the load on the working memory and providing us with *cognitive space* to focus on the activity (Wheatley et al., 2012).

But does the use of collaborative learning mean that the teacher no longer directs classroom activity or explicitly teaches anything? On the contrary, teachers have an important role to play in promoting positive collaboration and, according to Blatchford et al. (2003), there are four ways in which it can enhance the potential of collaborative learning activities.

1. Thinking about the content of group tasks to ensure that some of it will be perceived as 'fun'.

2. Scaffolding activities so that groups (and individuals) can work in constructive ways.

3. Transferring control of the learning to students so that the teacher's role is to guide rather than direct.

4. Structuring tasks carefully by providing a clear introduction and debriefing to ensure learners understand their roles and the purpose of the activity.

So while this methodology does indeed transfer more responsibility to learners it doesn't actually change the teacher's role in relation to planning and directing learning. Much like the conductor of an orchestra, the teacher has a fundamental role in leading and guiding the overall performance.

ACTIVITY 6.1

What type of activities could you use to enhance collaboration in your classroom? Make a list of potential tasks which could be incorporated into your teaching, then discuss these with your mentor so that you can select something to try out in your next class.

CASE STUDY

Milena's journal

So I gave it a go, I relinquished some of my control over my class and encouraged them to work collaboratively. I wanted to give them complete freedom so I designed a research task. I was careful not to try to control the activity too much and even gave them freedom to decide what they would research and how they would go about it. I put them into groups of three and set them free on the task - the only stipulation being that they had to be back in the class in 45 minutes.

It was a disaster! They exited the classroom at the speed of light, some said they were going to the library, others to the IT suite, but when I circulated to try to support them, I couldn't actually find any of them and then I received a complaint from the Head of Department saying that some of my students had been caught smoking in the toilets and most of the others were laughing and joking in the coffee bar! The ones who did try to complete the task did it so badly it was unlikely they would have learned anything from it. I knew it wasn't safe to let them have any freedom over their activities!

Learning in groups

The use of group work provides the tutor with an opportunity to introduce new learning in a non-directive way, allows learners to make their own constructs for new learning and has the potential to develop skills such as team working, communicating and organisation. This also supports the development of essential skills for learning and, according to Vygotsky, language itself promotes thinking so any instructional strategy which promotes literacy plays a fundamental role in knowledge construction (Vygotsky, 1978). The argument for employing forms of co-operative learning is a strong one but, as Milena discovered, group work still requires some direction from the teacher. Learners can be actively involved from the outset, for example you could negotiate aspects of the task with them, but, as a general rule, they will also require clear guidance about the scope and purpose of the task. By leaving this completely open, Milena had omitted to provide any structure and it is highly likely that her students were confused about what they were supposed to be doing.

Johnson and Johnson (1999) make reference to two types of co-operative learning: formal co-operative learning and informal co-operative learning. The latter consists of students working together to achieve a joint learning goal and may be used to focus their attention on a topic, set expectations about what will be covered in the class or perhaps sum up what has been covered. Formal co-operative learning involves students having a shared learning goal such as problem-solving or conducting a survey and completing specific tasks. In this case the teacher has made a number of decisions about how the learning will be structured and what its outcomes will be. Normally this will involve:

- setting objectives for the learning, such as task outcomes or the development of particular social skills;

- deciding on the size and make-up of the group, involving decisions such as whether or not groups should be self-selecting;

- explaining the task and the positive interdependence of the groups;

- monitoring students' learning and intervening to provide assistance where required;

- systematically observing and collecting data on how each group is working;

- assessing students' learning and helping students to think about how well their groups functioned.

PAUSE POINT

What are the key ingredients for successful classroom collaboration?

CASE STUDY

Milena's journal

This seems to have been quite a journey for me. My own reading and what I have been learning on the PGCE had convinced me of the power of classroom collaboration but I really wasn't prepared for how awry things could go! I thought it would simply be a case of giving the students more free-dom and being less controlling ... how wrong I was. I realised that this type of activity takes just as

(Continued)

(Continued)

much planning as traditional teaching and it is really important (perhaps even more important) to provide my students with the structure they need in order to complete group activities. That said, when I got it right the results were amazing. The students said how much they had enjoyed the activities, they were asking a lot more questions and were really beginning to think about their answers. In fact, I am so convinced about the power of co-operative learning that I am going to suggest we encourage the teachers to do it.

Collegiality and teacher collaboration

At the beginning of the chapter we considered the idea that 'collaboration' may be a misunderstood term. Often when people talk about collaborating with others, what they are really referring to are forms of collegiality, i.e. co-operation between colleagues who have a shared aim. In the example provided, reference was made to sharing resources and working side by side; examples of a collegiate working environment and probably key ingredients to create an environment of collaboration.

The main difference between collegiate and collaborative working is the overall focus of activity. When colleagues collaborate they have a distinct aim, they are working together to produce something. While this means that they will probably work side by side in supportive ways, it might also mean that there is an element of challenge to ensure that collaboration has a beneficial outcome.

Despite the potential benefits of collaboration, teacher collaboration is not a common phenomenon. Lortie (1975) described schools as *egg crates*, illustrating how teachers were kept apart and often worked in isolation. More recently, in the FE sector, this approach was described as *silo working*, to depict the separate nature of teacher activity defined by the subject they teach (Thompson and Wolstencroft, 2018). It would seem that working collaboratively is not necessarily something which happens that often and, according to Piercey (2010), this may be a response to how teams are structured and the ways in which collaboration is sometimes demanded rather than encouraged. When this approach is taken, collaborative activity is enforced and is unlikely to result in positive outcomes. But what should we do to stimulate teacher collaboration?

Figure 6.3 Teacher collaboration

PAUSE POINT

Based on your work or placement environment, what do you think stops teachers from collaborating on projects? What is your personal perspective on collaboration? Is there anything that would stop you from working collaboratively with your colleagues?

According to Friend and Cook (1992) there are six conditions required for effective collaboration; these are:

1. having mutual goals;

2. basing collaborative activity on voluntary relationships;

3. parity among participants;

4. sharing responsibility for participation and decision-making;

5. shared responsibility for outcomes;

6. sharing resources.

You may be able to add to this based on your reflections in the pause point. For many teachers 'time' is cited as the biggest obstacle to collaborative working. Indeed, this is likely to be cited as the reason for not taking part in any activity outside of the day-to-day requirements of the job, for example, attending continuing professional development (CPD) events or getting involved in research. Yet, some teachers do get involved in these activities, so presumably can find the time to do so. This may be due to different approaches to managing work and personal commitments and/ or priorities. Additional factors could relate to confidence in taking part in collaborative activities or even trusting that the activity will be beneficial to everybody.

Hattie and Zierer (2018) suggest that the mindframe and competences required for successful collaboration are things which need to be learned. For this learning to take place there are wider considerations which may be implemented at an organisation or department level, such as how and why collaborative teams are established. Collaboration requires the building of relationships as well as making time for collaborative activity and for these reasons is something which is most successful when embedded into the organisation culture. In terms of teacher collaboration, Hattie and Zierer outline a number of steps to co-operation.

1. Discussing with one another.

2. Supporting and criticising one another.

3. Planning and evaluating lessons together.

4. Delivering lessons together.

(2018, p35)

But these only focus on a small part of teacher activity (teaching lessons). The teacher's role is of course much wider than that, so collaborative activity could also encompass things such as curriculum planning, course development or research activity. Additional collaborative activities could take the form of:

- **peer observation** – providing an opportunity to observe each other's lessons as a form of sharing and adapting ideas;

- **action research projects** – usually involving small-scale research activity on an aspect of professional practice. This provides data for evaluation and, if required, further adaptation of approaches.

- **reading groups** – although not focussed on specific projects they may spark ideas for future developments. Reading groups are a starting point for discussion and may lead to a number of ideas for future projects.

Whatever form of collaborative activity is chosen it is important that this takes place in a supportive and blame-free environment in full acceptance that not every project will be successful.

Chapter summary

In this chapter we have considered the benefits of collaborative learning in the classroom and explored strategies you could employ to develop group work and co-operation. We have also discussed the important aspect of teacher collaboration, something which is often neglected.

MENTOR MOMENT

In this section we have included starter points for discussions with mentors to provide an opportunity for you to talk through the chapter content. The aim of the questions is to encourage you to interrogate your understanding of the concepts presented and consider ways in which these might influence your teaching.

- What are the potential benefits of introducing co-operative learning in the classroom?
- What might be the potential obstacles?
- What type of activities might work with your students?
- In what ways could you collaborate with your colleagues?

Suggested further reading

Gillies, RM, Ashman, AF, and Terwell, J (2008) *The Teacher's Role in Implementing Co-operative Learning in the Classroom.* New York: Springer.

Hattie, J and Zierer, K (2018) *10 Mindframes for Visible Learning: Teaching for Success.* Abingdon: Routledge.

References

Ashman, G (2018) *The Truth about Teaching: An Evidence-Informed Guide for New Teachers*. London: SAGE.

Bandura, A (1986) The explanatory and predictive scope of self-efficacy theory. *Journal of Clinical and Social Psychology*, 4 (3): 359–73.

Blatchford, P, Kutnick, P, Baines, E, and Galton, M (2003) Toward a social pedagogy of classroom group work. *International Journal of Educational Research*, 39 (1–2): 153–72.

Clinton, J, Cairns, K, Mclaren, P and Simpson, S (2014) Evaluation of the Victorian Deaf Education Institute Real-Time Captioning Pilot Program, Final Report, August 2014, The University of Melbourne: Centre for Program Evaluation.

Friend, M and Cook, L (1992) *Interactions: Collaboration Skills for School Professionals*. New York: Longman.

Gillies, RM, Ashman, AF, and Terwell, J (2008) *The Teacher's Role in Implementing Co-operative Learning in the Classroom*. New York: Springer.

Hattie, J (online) High impact strategies for teachers. Available at **www.teacherstoolbox. co.uk/T_effect_sizes.html** (Accessed 6 March 2019).

Hattie, J and Zierer, K (2018) *10 Mindframes for Visible Learning: Teaching for Success*. Abingdon: Routledge.

Johnson, DW and Johnson, RT (1999) Making cooperative learning work. *Theory into Practice*, 38 (2): 67–73.

Kolb, DA (1984) *Experiential Learning: Experience as a Source of Learning and Development*. Eaglewood Cliffs, NJ: Prentice Hall.

Littleton, K, Mercer, N, Dawes, L, Wegerif, R, Rowe, D and Sams, C (2005) Talking and thinking together at Key Stage 1. *Early Years*, 25 (2): 167–82.

Lortie, DC (1975) *Schoolteacher: A Sociological Study*. Chicago, IL: University of Chicago Press.

Miles, LK, Nind, LK, Henderson, Z and Macrae, CN (2010) Moving memories: behavioural synchrony and memory for self and others. *Journal of Experimental Social Psychology*, 46 (2): 457–60.

Piercey, D (2010) Why don't teachers collaborate? A leadership conundrum. Available at **https://bettereducate.com/uploads/file/40949_CollaborationTime_40665Why DontTeachersCollaborateALeadershipConundrumWhyDontTeachersCollaborate.pdf** (Accessed 3 March 2019).

Rogers, C (1969) *Freedom to Learn: A View of What Education Might Become*. Ohio: C. E. Merrill Publishing Company.

Sharratt, LD and Planche, BM (2016) *Leading Collaborative Learning: Empowering Excellence*. London: SAGE.

Thompson, C and Wolstencroft, P (2018) No more superheroes – only Avatars? – survival role play in English post compulsory education, in Merrill, B, Galimberti, A, Nizinska, A and

González-Monteagudo, J (eds) *Continuity and Discontinuity in Learning Careers, Potentials for a Learning Space in a Changing World*. Leiden, The Netherlands/Boston, MA: Brill, Sense.

Vygotsky, LS (1978) *Mind in Society: The Development of Higher Psychological Processes*. Cambridge, MA: Harvard University Press.

Wheatley, T, Kang, O, Parkinson, C and Looser, CE (2012) From mind perception to mental connection: synchrony as a mechanism for social understanding. *Social and Personality Psychology Compass*, 6 (8): 589–606.

7

CO-CONSTRUCTING LEARNING

In this chapter we will explore:

- what is meant by humanism;
- the principles of humanist teaching and learning;
- the connection between humanism and other theories;
- some of the theorists connected with humanism;
- how humanism can be applied in the classroom.

Introduction

Humanism is probably one of the most widely used and least understood theories of teaching and learning. Emerging in the 1960s, humanism is a contentious theory when applied to teaching, being loved by some teachers as it is based on principles which place the students firmly at the heart of the learning process, it is abhorred by others as a 'pink and fluffy' theory with little relevance to classroom practice. Nevertheless, it can be argued that all teachers are to some extent humanists in that most come into the teaching profession with a desire to develop students to their full potential in some way or another. For many teachers their aspirations are not simply focussed on supporting students to understand subject matter but on developing the students in other ways, supporting them to become fully rounded human beings, replete with the characteristics, beliefs, values and attitudes which will enable them to become useful members of society. In some respects, the place of humanism in teaching and learning can be summed up as ensuring that students don't only have the tools (the knowledge and skills) to *be* someone, but gain the tools to understand themselves so that they are able to *become* someone.

In this chapter we meet Bobby, an enthusiastic teacher who has worked as a design engineer previously and is now teaching maths to students in a fairly traditional inner-city secondary school with a culturally diverse student population. The students that Bobby teach range from 11 to 18 years of age.

Figure 7.1 Bobby's story

Bobby's journal

There was a really interesting discussion in the staffroom at lunchtime. The school counsellor argued that teachers have a moral responsibility to develop every student as a person whereas some of the teachers saw their role mainly as being connected with getting students through their exams. I think it might be a bit of both! The counsellor was banging on about humanism and humanistic teaching so I might have a look at that and see what I think.

Bobby's journal

Well, I've had a look through the textbooks and as far as I can see there are five principles underlying humanistic teaching and learning.

1. *Humanist educators argue that students learn best in an environment in which they feel safe. When a student feels secure they learn more easily and the learning is more meaningful to the individual.*

2. *In education, humanists regard the primary responsibilities of educators and the education system itself to be the fostering of the desire to learn within the individual and to teach students how they can learn while inspiring within them a yearning to learn independently.*

3. *Humanists believe that learning should be self-directed – the individual should not only take responsibility for their learning, but should also be responsible for choosing what and how they learn and how they present their understanding.*

4. *Humanistic education contends that in addition to acquiring knowledge and skills in meaning-making, the feelings of students play an important part in the learning process. Whereas most traditional education practice tended to separate the cognitive and affective domains, humanistic education seeks to combine them.*

5. *Humanists argue that the only form of evaluation that is of any real value is the process of self-evaluation carried out by the individual who assesses the value and usefulness of the learning to them as a person.*

Now all I have got to do is see how they apply to my professional practice; promoting a safe learning environment is pretty axiomatic when you think about it, but some of the other points might be worth trying out. I need to have a good look at them one at a time and see how they fit with my classes. OK – here goes with the first one – a safe environment.

A safe environment

It would seem from the comment, *a safe environment for learning is pretty axiomatic*, that Bobby is familiar with the work of Maslow and his theory of the Hierarchy of Needs (1954), in which he argues that a range of student needs must be met before they can self-actualise. Bobby notes that, nowadays, schools and teachers generally go out of their way to ensure that the students' basic physiological, safety and love/belonging needs (the deficiency needs) are met. In Bobby's school there are policies and practices to ensure that students have regular breaks, access to refreshment, work in inclusive settings that are friendly and emotionally and physically safe, and that individual students are included in all learning activities. However, when Bobby looks for guidance in the form of school policies to facilitate the top two tiers of the hierarchy there are only general mission statements. From this, Bobby concludes that the top two elements – self-esteem and self-actualisation (the growth needs) – of the traditional five-step hierarchy are something which need to be thought about and implemented by the teacher, rather than something which can be legislated for by the institution. (Incidentally, you might find in your research more complex models of the hierarchy of needs – several other steps have been added to the pyramid both by Maslow and subsequent theorists.)

In exploring the concept of 'growth needs' Bobby finds the work of Carl Rogers of particular interest. Rogers (1959) contends that all humans have an inbuilt desire to achieve their full potential and become a fully functioning person – to self-actualise in Maslow's terms. To become a fully functioning person, Rogers argued that individuals had to have a positive self-image, an image of themselves which is created by congruence between their personal feelings of self-worth or self-esteem and the feeling that they are positively perceived and valued as individuals by others. To foster development in any educational setting the learning environment has to be both positive and constructive, but to ensure that the students feel valued and respected so that they are able to grow on a personal as well as an academic level, Rogers identified three key factors.

1. Empathy (knowing that their views and thoughts are being heard and understood by the teacher and peers).

2. Acceptance (being accepted by others for what they are without being judged) – what Rogers described as unconditional positive regard, but which we would now probably describe as unconditional respect.

3. Genuineness (the feeling that they can be open with teachers and peers with their views, feelings and beliefs).

If these three elements are present in the classroom the student will feel secure in the knowledge that they will be able to try new things out and the respect they receive as an individual from peers and teachers will not be withdrawn if they make mistakes.

PAUSE POINT

Think about the three key factors identified by Rogers. How do you think that Bobby could introduce these factors into the classroom? Think about your own teaching - how could you use them as part of your professional practice as a teacher?

Bobby decides to try out some new teaching techniques with the younger students who can be a bit of a handful at times. One of the things Bobby tries is giving each student five tokens. Each time the student wants to speak in a class discussion or answer a question from the teacher they have to surrender a token; once they have used their tokens they are not allowed to speak again. Bobby also insists that students are quiet while other students are speaking and that if they want to challenge any-thing another student is saying they have to give a reason or provide some evidence to support their view rather than just stating their position. By using this exercise Bobby ensures that every student knows that their answers or views are being heard by their peers and that making (and stating) snap judgements about either the speaker or the point they are making is discouraged. Having introduced this system Bobby finds that the students interact more positively and that less confident students feel more able to participate fully in class activities.

CASE STUDY

Bobby's journal

Well that worked OK - it took a bit of time for them to get the hang of it but the students are becoming more aware of each other and how they can interact more positively and are beginning to treat each other with more respect. What I have found, however, is that this only works if the students are interested so maybe my New Year's resolution needs to be that I need to ensure my students are motivated.

Fostering a desire to learn

Teaching to motivate and inspire student learning is an essential component in the humanist tradition of teaching and learning, and has already been explored in some depth in Chapter 4. Motivation, however, is a personal phenomenon; what arouses the interest of one student may not have the same effect on another. Modelling ways of meaning-making or participating in interactive, inclusive activities which facilitate the incorporation of new knowledge into existing schema (Piaget, 1936) or in building new ones using constructivist teaching methods (see Chapter 5) are established methods of motivating students. However, Knowles et al. (2005), although concentrating primarily on androgogic theory (a learning theory more usually connected with adult learners), suggest that students are more likely to be motivated if they are able to concentrate on subjects which they regard as being relevant to their immediate or future needs.

ACTIVITY 7.1

Go back to Chapter 4 and review how motivational theory can be implemented in the classroom. Think about the last point made above, that students can be motivated if they concentrate on things which they regard as being relevant to their immediate or future needs.

- How do you think that Bobby could use this in teaching maths?
- How could you incorporate this means of motivating students in your professional practice as a teacher?

Bobby decides to try to make mathematical theory more relevant to the students but quickly realises that the motivation for learning needs to be tailored to the group being taught. For the younger students, who are learning how to calculate the volumes of different shapes, Bobby decides to teach them how to calculate the volume of a cylinder by measuring empty drinks cans and then inserting their measurements into the formula. To provide extra motivation Bobby uses different empty cans and teaches the students how to work out which is the best value for money. For older students, who are coming up to their exams, Bobby decides to introduce a ten-minute revision session at the end of each lesson to make sure that the students are up to speed on the formulae and practices which they will need for the exam. By taking a different approach to each group of students Bobby is ensuring that the motivator matches the needs of the students.

— **CASE STUDY** —

Bobby's journal

Well it looks like it's a case of 'horses for courses' when it comes to motivation. If the students can see the point of doing something then they are more interested, and they learn more easily if they can see a practical application. Onwards and upwards! I'm not so sure about the next point that I found about humanist theory – self-directed learning might be a bit trickier than it looks with some of my groups of students.

Self-directed learning

Closely allied to the theory expounded by Knowles et al., that motivation can be engendered by appealing to personal interest, is Candy's (1991) theory of self-directed learning. For Candy, learning is an independent pursuit conducted at an individual level rather than the product of the collaborative processes advocated by constructivism (see Chapter 5). To learn effectively, he argues, students need to be able to exercise personal autonomy (although the level of autonomy will vary according to the individual's current level of knowledge and the context), self-management and control not only of the choice of subject but also the manner of their learning. The thesis of self-directed learning has become increasingly relevant with the inception of the digital era, where students are able to research independently and find information with ease by using the internet, which offers them vastly increased opportunities to follow their personal interests.

PAUSE POINT

As Candy notes, the level of personal autonomy in learning varies according to the individual, the context and their current level of knowledge. Bobby teaches students of different ages with diverse levels of maturity and diverse motivations. How feasible do you think it is for Bobby to implement this theory with students? Think about your own classes – how do you think you could give your students an appropriate level of autonomy in learning?

Personal autonomy in learning varies according to the individual. What measures do you think Bobby could take to increase student autonomy? What could you do in your professional practice to make your students more autonomous learners?

Bobby decides to take a differentiated approach in granting autonomy to students. With the younger students she makes a point of offering them a limited amount of choice, letting them choose between two or three different ways of learning which will lead to the same end-point. Bobby christens this option 'guided choice' – the students feel they have some level of autonomy and are consequently more willing to participate as they feel as though they can exercise some control over their learning. For the older learners, Bobby decides to set projects which students can do independently and then come together as a group to discuss their findings. This gives students the feeling that they can control not only the subject matter that they have to learn but also the manner in which they gain and share information.

CASE STUDY

Bobby's journal

Well, giving the younger students access to 'guided choice' seems to work reasonably well but not quite as well as I would like it to. It seems to take a long time for them to decide which option they are going to take - maybe I need to think about the options themselves and, in future, make them more narrow and focussed. With the older students, giving them a 'buy-in' to the way in which they learn has worked really well - they are much more motivated and the diverse information that they are gathering through their research is really useful in starting discussions when they are comparing notes. What I have noticed, however, is that some students really don't like the system, they feel that they want their learning to be more directed and I need to be able to take account of this in my teaching.

The importance of feelings and emotions

From this entry it looks as though Bobby has encountered the fourth point from the second journal entry – the need to take account of the feelings and emotions of students in humanistic teaching and learning. The majority of learning theory concentrates on the cognitive aspects of learning with particular reference to the practicalities and processes of learning. Humanists such as Rogers (1959), however, viewed education as a holistic process intended to foster the development of the whole person rather than just the intellectual capacity of the individual, and noted the effects of the affective domain on the response of students in the cognitive domain.

Since the early 1990s when Salovey and Mayer coined the term emotional intelligence (EI), there has been an increased interest in the management of the emotional response of students to learning. EI was initially seen (relatively) simply as the cognitive process which allowed individuals to recognise and control their own feelings and emotions and to identify the emotional responses of others. By identifying the emotional response in others they were able to use them to guide their personal responses to people and situations. Goleman (1996) extended the notion of EI to include the individual's social response to emotion in addition to their purely psychological response, arguing that EI consisted of five interrelated elements: self-awareness, self-regulation, internal motivation, empathy and social skills. By understanding (self-awareness) and controlling their own emotions (self-regulation) and responding appropriately to others (empathy), individuals, he argued, would be able to manage relationships more successfully (social skills) and would ultimately be able to achieve their (internally motivated) personal and social objectives.

Taking into account the feelings and emotions of students is probably the most 'pink and fluffy' aspect of humanism. As human beings, the majority of us have an innate ability to 'read' the emotional state of others and react accordingly. Students who feel threatened in any way are likely to resort to negative patterns of behaviour, but humanist teaching methods can support students to think about their responses rather than simply acting negatively. An emotionally intelligent classroom is one that is likely to be a constructive and happy setting for teaching and learning. However, it's very easy when faced with an emotionally vulnerable student for the teacher to become conflicted between a desire to befriend and support the student and maintaining a professional distance between themselves and the student, and this is something about which the emotionally intelligent teacher must remain cognisant.

PAUSE POINT

As we've noted previously, Bobby teaches students of different ages with diverse levels of maturity. How do you think Bobby should try to make the classroom more emotionally intelligent for young students? What steps should Bobby take to make the classroom more emotionally intelligent?

One of the ways that Bobby decides to try to develop an emotionally intelligent classroom with younger students is by encouraging them to 'own' the learning process by involving them in creating the rules which will govern their behaviour in the classroom. By showing respect for the views and feelings of students Bobby is empowering them, making them feel valued and appreciated. Later, Bobby decides to build on this feeling of empowerment by allowing the same students a limited degree of participation in deciding how they learn, choosing to work on tasks in groups or as individuals to achieve specific objectives, as an integral part of the learning process. When working with the older students, to take account of individual preferences in ways of learning (in groups, pairs, individually, using information technology, working in the library, etc.), where possible Bobby increases the level of personal autonomy for the students by introducing challenging, focussed, research-based activities and discussing the outcome with individuals and groups. By exploring reasons for the activities, helping students identify what it is they feel they have learned and how their learning fits in with their current understandings, views and beliefs, Bobby is acknowledging their maturity and making them feel valued and respected.

CASE STUDY

Bobby's journal

OK, this seems to be working reasonably well with all the groups of students and is very much appreciated by the older students in particular. The younger ones sometimes seem as though they want to spend more time deciding how they learn rather than actually learning and I am a bit concerned that they sometimes remember the activity itself rather than the point of the activity. I need to do something about this to make sure they understand why they are doing something and what they are supposed to be learning and not just that they are having fun.

Evaluating learning

Bobby is quite right in supposing that sometimes students remember the learning activity itself rather than the purpose of the activity, and the final point that Bobby identified when she was researching humanist theory (and possibly one of the most important ones) was the need for individual evaluation of learning. Learning is usually regarded as something which can be measured, however, in humanist theory the informal, unintentional and unstructured learning which forms part of the individual's development into a *fully functioning person* (Rogers, 1959) also needs to be taken into account. Unlike learning in the cognitive domain, learning in the affective domain is something which may be taken for granted or even unacknowledged by the student themselves and active, directed reflection (possibly initiated by the teacher) may be needed in order for the student to identify that learning has taken place. Models of reflective practice (Schön, 1974 in Smith, 2011, and Ullmann 2015) used by teachers have been discussed in Chapter 1; however, reflection is also an important and integral part of the learning process for students.

Reflective models are frequently based on answering three, ostensibly straightforward, questions: 'what?', 'so what?' and 'now what?' In answering the 'what' question students are asked to identify the tangible aspects occurring in a situation: what it was they were trying to achieve, what the response of others was and any consequences of the situation. In the 'so what' stage of the analysis the student is challenged to consider what it is that they have learned by asking themselves to identify what they learned, what they were thinking and feeling at the time, whether they had any other knowledge that could have been brought into the situation and whether they now have a new or different under- standing of the situation they have experienced. The last element, the 'now what' aspect, asks students to think about change: what needs to be done to improve the situation, any wider issues that might need to be considered to make the situation more successful, anything they might do differently in the future and any consequences of their actions.

One of the best known reflective cycles that can be used by students to identify informal serendipi- tous learning in the affective domain is that offered by Gibbs (1988). This model extends the 'what, so what, now what' model by asking the user to evaluate the relevance and importance of the learn- ing at a personal level and humanists, as Bobby notes in the early entry in the journal, believe that *the only form of evaluation that is of any real value is the process of self-evaluation carried out by the indi- vidual who assesses the value and usefulness of the learning to them as a person.*

ACTIVITY 7.2

Not all students find reflection easy – many have been taught to associate learning with the retention of facts, concepts and ideas, and the notion of personal development and growth as something which might be learned as part of classroom practice in addition to facts, theories and concepts is some- thing which is somewhat alien to them. Jot down your ideas about what Bobby could do to make students aware of the wider aspects of their learning. Do you think different techniques might be needed for different age groups? How would you encourage reflection among the student you teach?

Bobby decides that teaching reflective practice to young students will help them not only to make connections with previous learning but will also help them in the meaning-making process when confronted with new information/knowledge. One of the things which Bobby decides to try with his younger students is introducing a whole class discussion at the end of the lesson. All the stu- dents are encouraged to participate in this by saying what they think they have learned and Bobby helps the discussion along by asking a series of challenging questions that encourage students to think more widely about the lesson and learning and identify any changes in their attitudes, views or beliefs. Bobby finds, much as expected, that the older students are better at reflecting on their own learning although they still tend to concentrate on the subject matter rather than the wider aspects of learning, and at times it would appear that their attitudes are more entrenched and more difficult to challenge than those of younger students. When this happens, Bobby encourages individuals or small groups (depending on the situation) to discuss the attitudes which have been expressed with their peers, using some general questions or comments to help steer the discussion if necessary. Through reflection, discussion and interaction with others in a classroom setting, Bobby encourages students to critically examine their prior interpretations and assumptions about a topic and discover new meanings and understandings.

CASE STUDY

Bobby's journal

Well – introducing humanism into my teaching has proved to be an interesting experiment. It hasn't always worked – some students still want to concentrate solely on the subject, but the younger ones are getting the hang of it and I've noticed a big change in them both in terms of their behaviour and attitude in class. The older ones were a bit more resistant – probably because they had never been taught like this (it is a fairly traditional school!) but they are communicating with each other more and are much more open to challenging the attitudes and findings of their peers and of having their thoughts and ideas challenged by others. All part of the growth process!

What Bobby has noticed about the changes in attitude among his students would be described by Mezirow (2000) as transformative learning. For Mezirow, learning is a holistic process concerned with personal change in the individual's underlying values and beliefs which is brought about by the introduction of four major factors.

1. Disorientating dilemmas (the activities and questions that Bobby has posed in teaching which have challenged the individual's assumptions and values).

2. Critical reflection (questioning of the initial assumptions through reflection).

3. Rational dialogue (discussion, and having views and beliefs challenged by peers and teachers in a non-threatening atmosphere).

4. Action (the action taken by an individual in refining or elaborating their existing frames of reference).

For the sake of completeness I am going to introduce the views of the Brazilian philosopher Paulo Freire. His view on education, which he describes as liberation pedagogy, extends the theory of humanist education and introduces a political perspective which is not normally associated with formal education. For Freire, education is a tool for the transformation of the individual both politically and socially; education is either:

> *an instrument which is used to … bring about conformity, or … the practice of freedom. … [Education becomes the] … means by which … [students] … deal critically with reality and discover how to participate in the transformation of their world.*
>
> (Freire, 2007, p34)

In Freire's view, education allows students to see, understand and challenge the ways in which society shapes the way students perceive themselves and their world. By understanding and reflecting on this understanding students should be able to recognise how it can be changed.

PAUSE POINT ───────────────────────

Do you agree with Freire's views?

Chapter summary

In this chapter we have looked at what is meant by humanism and how this contentious theory fits in with other, more conventional, theories of education. We have examined the five principles of humanist teaching and learning and how they can be incorporated into classroom practice. Some of the main theorists connected with humanism have been discussed and the connections and differences which exist between them.

MENTOR MOMENT ───────────────────

Humanism as a theory of education is contentious, although it could be argued that all teachers who wish to develop students to their full potential have humanist tendencies. Think about the following questions and discuss them with your mentor.

- How appropriate is constructivist teaching for the students you teach?
- What steps could you take to incorporate humanism into your teaching?
- What do you think the benefits of humanist teaching would be for you and your students?
- How do you think your students would react to being taught in this way?

── **Suggested further reading** ────────────────

Knowles, MS, Holton, EF and Swanson, RA (2005) *The Adult Learner* (8th ed). Abingdon: Routledge.

Smith, MK (2011) Donald Schön: learning, reflection and change. *The Encyclopedia of Informal Education*. Available at **www.infed.org/thinkers/et-schon.htm** (Accessed 28 February 2019).

── **References** ━━━━━━━━━━━━━━━━━━━

Candy, PC (1991) *Self-Direction for Lifelong Learning*. San Francisco, CA: Jossey-Bass.

Freire, P (2007) *Pedagogy of the Oppressed*. New York: Continuum.

Gibbs, G (1988) *Learning by Doing: A Guide to Teaching and Learning Methods*. Oxford: Further Education Unit, Oxford Polytechnic.

Goleman, **D** (1996) *Emotional Intelligence: Why It Can Matter More than IQ.* London: Bloomsbury.

Knowles, **MS**, **Holton**, **EF and Swanson**, **RA** (2005) *The Adult Learner* (8th ed). Abingdon: Routledge.

Maslow, **AH** (1954) *Motivation and Personality.* New York: Harper & Row.

Mezirow, **J** (2000) *Learning as Transformation: Critical Perspectives on a Theory in Progress.* San Francisco, CA: Jossey-Bass.

Piaget, **J** (1936) *Origins of Intelligence in the Child.* London: Routledge & Kegan Paul.

Rogers, **C** (1959) A theory of therapy, personality and interpersonal relationships as developed in the client-centered framework, in Koch, S (ed) *Psychology: A Study of a Science. Volume 3: Formulations of the Person and the Social Context.* New York: McGraw Hill.

Salovey, **P and Mayer**, **JD** (1990) Emotional intelligence. *Imagination, Cognition, and Personality*, 9 (3): 185–211.

Smith, **MK** (2011) Donald Schön: learning, reflection and change. *The Encyclopedia of Informal Education.* Available at **www.infed.org/thinkers/et-schon.htm** (Accessed 28 February 2019).

Ullmann, **TD** (2015) 'Automated detection of reflection in texts: a machine learning based approach (PhD thesis)'. The Open University, Milton Keynes [online]. Available at **https://pdfs.semantic-scholar.org/d5f2/e9966dd73cba5312380aef89ec9f571239ab.pdf**

8

MIXING IT UP

In this chapter we will explore:

- what we mean by 'mixing it up';
- mixing it up to meet the needs of students;
- combining elements to form a cohesive whole;
- using mixed up theory in the classroom to improve teaching and learning.

Introduction

In the words of the old adage 'one swallow does not a summer make', applying one theory in the classroom generally doesn't make for good teaching and learning. Students are all individuals; they all have different needs, expectations, talents and abilities, not to mention each having their own way of making meaning, learning style (if there is any such thing – see Chapter 1) and motivation for learning. When confronted with a class of up to 30 students, teaching is made into a complicated process guaranteed to stretch the ability of any teacher. Regrettably, nothing works every time in a classroom. The theories so painstakingly applied by the teacher when constructing the learning objectives and activities, which worked wonderfully with one group of students, may prove totally ineffective when applied to a different group, requiring the teacher to make some very rapid adjustments to the lesson plan in order for learning to take place.

Taking students' different needs and abilities into account to ensure that they are all included in the learning process is not an easy matter. As most of us find out fairly early in our teaching careers, one size does not fit all, and not every student is able to meet the learning objectives through the use of a specific activity or teaching method. Just as we need to differentiate the teaching methods and activities we use in our classroom practice in order to meet the needs of our students and help them to learn effectively, so we need to differentiate the learning theories that we apply in planning, delivering and assessing teaching and learning.

Embedded in the introduction to this chapter are two very important concepts – inclusion and differentiation. Teachers are constantly being told that they must differentiate so that they 'teach to each' in order to ensure that every student is included in learning and has full access to the curriculum. This, however, presents teachers with the seemingly impossible task of planning to meet the needs of their students on an individual basis. Although they are possibly two of the most overworked and confused (and confusing) concepts in any teachers' theoretical canon, an understanding of how inclusion and differentiation can be implemented in classroom practice retains a critically important position in the process of teaching and learning. To meet the needs of (the generally very mixed) groups of students that teachers are likely to have to work with, it is helpful if teachers can adopt elements from different theories and weave them together to develop a cohesive strategy which will help them to meet the learning needs of individual students.

In this chapter we meet Casey, a young teacher of English and humanities. He is new to teaching in a secondary school environment, having just moved from a college which specialised in vocational education to a secondary school with a sixth form where students take BTEC and A level qualifications. Casey will be teaching English A level and BTEC humanities. Casey has also been asked, for the first time, to take on a formal pastoral role for a group of students.

CASE STUDY

Casey's journal

New term, new school, new class. I've just taught the new humanities group for the third time. They seem a very 'mixed bag', but some of the teachers who have worked with them previously have given me a bit of a 'heads up' on one or two of them which might be helpful. The only things they seem to have in common is that they are all working towards the same qualification, they are more or less the same age (but from what I have seen so far not the same level of maturity in terms of behaviour!) and they are all bundled into one class. The problem I seem to be facing is that while they are all working towards the same qualification they are working at different levels, and to compound the issue some of them have transferred in from other schools where they have been taught in different ways, so there are some very different expectations of teaching and learning. All classes of students are a mixed bunch, I accept that, but this group seem to be more of a mixture than I expected in a school.

I have been told by the staff there are a couple of 'slow readers', another who is reluctant to interact with other students; one who was described, by another member of staff who worked with him last year, as being 'pretty bright but with the attention span of a butterfly' and who can be a bit disruptive if not fully occupied most of the time; and a little group who have been labelled 'just plain lazy'. In addition to the 'heads up' from the staff the group profile shows that there are some students who are going to need some additional support one way or another but don't qualify for formal support under an EHCP. Overall they seem like a nice group but they are so noisy and all some of them seem to want to do is chat away between themselves, whatever I am doing. I suppose in many respects this is just a normal group of 16 to 17 year olds, but I do need to find a way of stretching my teaching so that they all learn effectively.

Figure 8.1 Casey's story

ACTIVITY 8.1

Having read the journal entry describing the class, list the main problems that you think Casey will have to overcome in teaching the group.

Some of the difficulties which you may have identified are as follows.

- Single level of qualification but students with very different entry levels.

- Students with variable experience and expectations of teaching and learning.

- Some students needing additional support due to behavioural issues, some with literacy issues, others with limited attentions spans, and so on.

- Students previously identified by other staff as being 'lazy'.

- Noisy students who do not give the teacher their attention.

You may well have identified other problem areas in the journal entry and you will also probably be thinking that this is a pretty normal group of students; in fact, you may already have had to teach a similar group in your professional practice. One thing, however, that is noted in the journal is that Casey has already listened to the opinions of various members of staff about the students in the group. While the opinions of other teachers can be very valuable, the wholesale adoption of their views can also be hazardous when teachers who have not worked with those students before are forming their initial opinions about individuals or groups. Becker (1973, p9), in his discussion on labelling theory, argues that groups and individuals *create deviance by making rules whose infraction creates deviance*. In terms of the classroom, the student who is labelled 'lazy' or 'disruptive' or a 'slow reader' may simply be the one who does not conform to the expectations of a particular teacher. However, as Goffman (1963) suggests, by having been given a 'label' which is likely to remain with them throughout their school career, the student may become stigmatised by others (teachers and peers alike) who see the label rather than the student. The acceptance of such a label by a student can significantly impact not only on the development of the student's personal self-image (Rogers, 1959) and behaviour in class, but also influence the behaviour of their peers towards the student and the learning process.

Creating coherence

As Casey's journal indicates this is a new group with a wide range of students, some of whom will inevitably be in a new environment and yet to establish personal relationships with their peers. To compound this there are a number of students from other institutions who will probably hold different expectations of the course, the teaching and the teacher. In order to build cohesive group identity Casey might initially consider adopting some approaches which lie within the humanist tradition. Casey might think about implementing activities which will allow students to experience two of the three lower levels of Maslow's (1943) theory of the Hierarchy of Needs: 'safety' and 'belonging'. In terms of safety, Casey could decide to encourage the class to agree their own rules of behaviour so that all students are not only aware of what is, and what is not, acceptable but are more likely to 'buy into' the rules having participated in their development. Casey could also make it clear that the classroom is an emotionally safe environment in which students can take risks when expressing their opinions or discussing topics in groups, although students should also be made aware that their views could be challenged by their peers. To encourage 'belonging' and avoid the potential 'ghettoisation' (Dyson, 2001) of some students (particularly those with special educational needs and/or disabilities), Casey could opt to use small group work to encourage interaction and integration. However, as Tuckman (1965) indicates, group formation will take time (and may prove to be a tempestuous process), so Casey might opt to design or 'engineer' groups (Mills and Alexander, 2013) in the classroom. In designing the groups Casey might decide to adopt, and by combining roles to suit the groups or meet the needs of individual students quite possibly amend, the team roles approach advocated by Belbin (2004).

Other processes that Casey might want to consider when working towards establishing an atmosphere of intellectual safety for students can be drawn from different schools of theory. For example, the use of advance organisers (Ausubel, 1960) which can forewarn students about the planned content and structure of learning is taken from the constructivist school. Within the advance organisers Casey could elect to incorporate elements from behaviourist theory by setting SMART, differentiated and measurable objectives for students (see Chapter 3), so that all students are confident that they can achieve within the lesson and will feel included in the learning process from the start of the lesson.

Planning for inclusion and differentiation

CASE STUDY

Casey's journal

Well, today we were having a look at the concept of poverty in the humanities class and in spite of my carefully constructed lesson plan it didn't quite go the way I wanted it to. By the end of the lesson some of them had 'got it' but some of them just didn't seem to have any idea at all. The trouble seems to be that some, but not all of them, have previous knowledge of the subjects having done GCSE or BTEC courses, but their understandings of the concepts are different and very patchy. The ones who had come across the main concepts of poverty became very bored quickly and started chatting among themselves (again!) and some of the others who hadn't hit these concepts before just seem to have given up. Coming to terms with any sort of theoretical concept is difficult for students but they will all need to understand the principal concepts for the assignment.

PAUSE POINT

What do you think that Casey could do to include and engage the students in the learning process?

Building the foundations for learning

The processes and theories which underpin the development of syllabi and planning individual lessons have been discussed in Chapter 3. In that chapter the need for building a firm foundation of knowledge, from which students can begin to make meaning for themselves by constructing their own ways of understandings, was stressed. It was suggested that for some students there might be a natural progression from behaviourist methods which laid the foundations of knowledge, to a more constructivist mode of learning by using cognitive teaching techniques to scaffold their progress across the Zone of Proximal Development (Vygotsky, 1978) to enable individuals to construct new knowledge. In theory, this move from a behaviourist form of learning through cognitivism to constructivism forms a continuum; however, as Casey noted in the initial journal entry, although the students *are all working towards the same qualification they are working at different levels* and the individual student's progression along this continuum is likely to be uneven and erratic.

Bruner (1960) suggested the use of a spiral curriculum, a method whereby the subject matter is revisited on a number of occasions. By increasing the complexity of the subject matter on each 'visit', students are able to develop their individual schemas (Piaget, 1936) by establishing firm relationships between new concepts and ideas introduced in the lessons and their existing knowledge and understanding. Casey could consider adapting this process to meet the needs of the students within the cohort by arranging a series of activities related to the same subject matter.

Including the students

Following some preparatory work with the whole class to establish a firm foundation of knowledge about the topic, three or four well-chosen questions could have been given to the students which required them to reflect on, evaluate and assess their personal level of knowledge and understanding of the subject. The students could then have been divided into three groups based on the students' responses or the teacher could have elected to follow the humanist tradition of allowing the students to self-select the group they would join on the basis of their perceived level of knowledge. Once this had been done differentiated exercises designed to suit the needs of each group could have been set. For example, using carefully selected pieces of written text, videos, podcasts, etc. which contained all the relevant information about the theoretical concepts of poverty, Casey could have:

* asked one group of students (those who Casey felt 'didn't seem to have any idea at all' about the subject) to work as a group to identify different definitions of poverty within the texts;

* tasked the group who felt they had a basic knowledge of the theoretical concepts to analyse the texts and in pairs or triads to locate examples of each of the basic principles within the texts before reporting back to their group;

* set an exercise for those who had felt they had a good understanding of the theories and principles associated with poverty to research where and how these principles can be used to explain poverty in current contexts.

Once the students had completed these tasks Casey could have asked each of the groups to present their findings to the whole class in sequence, working from the group who had identified basic things to the group that was working fairly independently to identify principles in practice in alternative contexts.

ACTIVITY 8.2

Look at the differentiated tasks listed above and using what you have learned so far, list the different theories that have been included.

Mixing and matching theories

Before starting any teaching the current level of knowledge and understanding of the students needs to be established. It was suggested that Casey could have achieved this by asking the students to answer a series of questions. In doing this Casey would have been working within the cognitive paradigm, asking individuals to reflect there and then (reflection in action – Schön, 1991) and assess their current schema (Piaget, 1936) relating to the concepts of poverty. Casey could then have integrated some elements of constructivism, giving the students a degree of personal autonomy by encouraging them to use their assessment to make a personal decision about the level of group they wish to join. In doing so, Casey would have provided an opportunity for students to engage in a level of self-direction (Candy, 1991). By using this type of approach Casey could not only have shown the students that their group and individual growth needs (Rogers, 1959) were being taken into account by the teacher, but could also have enabled the students to participate in, and take responsibility for, their own learning. By promoting student participation and engagement in the learning process, Casey could, in terms of Berne's (1961) theory of transactional analysis, have indicated to the students not only that their opinions were both valued and accepted by a *More Knowledgeable Other* (Vygotsky, 1978), but that the relationship between teacher and student was intended to be one of 'adult to adult' rather than 'adult to child' or 'parent to child', a tactic which would have increased their readiness to learn (Berne, 1961).

Dividing the cohort into smaller groups with targeted tasks and outcomes could have enabled Casey to make learning a social rather than a pedagogic process (Vygotsky, 1978; Bandura, 1977; Bruner, 1960). By encouraging students to not only communicate with, but to learn with and from, their peers in a social setting which encourages discussion and debate, can enable students to become actively engaged in the process of meaning-making and constructing new knowledge in ways which are unique to them. Casey could have developed this process in the latter stages of the lesson when the suggested exercise indicates that each group of students would be asked to present their findings to the whole class. Taking feedback sequentially, starting with the group who were asked to identify concepts in the texts through to those who were challenged to develop their higher level thinking skills (Bloom et al., 1956) to synthesise information by evaluating the validity of the concepts within different contexts, would have enabled all the students to learn within the cognitive domain. Every student would be receiving the same information which would have been 'chunked' into bite-size pieces by the groups as they fed back their findings to the class. However, students in the final group to present to the class who had to research new information would also have been challenged to work within the constructivist paradigm. Initially, they would have had to find information for themselves (discovery learning) and later, when giving feedback to the class, they would be using their findings to scaffold the developing understanding of their peers (Bruner, 1960). Grounding theory in this way helps students to connect abstract concepts with practice to either create new schema or absorb theory into their existing schema. By making the connection between theory and practice through the whole class participating in either confirming or expanding individuals' understanding of the concepts, all students would be able to begin to establish firm connections between episteme and phronesis (Korthagen and Kessels, 1999).

Using groups in learning

In the process of encouraging students to work in groups to build shared understandings, some students (as Casey noted in the journal entry) inevitably grasp concepts faster than others. Working together in groups could encourage the more advanced students to act as informal mentors helping their peers cross the *Zone of Proximal Development* (Vygotsky, 1978) by scaffolding (Bruner, 1960) their developing understanding by offering alternative explanations which facilitate reflection, discussion and challenge in an informal environment. In promoting interaction in these social settings the role of the teacher could change from that of pedagogue to that of being a collaborator in the construction of knowledge for students working more independently, while remaining as a guide and facilitator for other students who are working at the level of cognitivism rather than constructivism.

PAUSE POINT

After Casey's initial journal entry you were asked to list the main problems that you think Casey will have to overcome in teaching the group. How do you think that using a differentiated lesson would address the difficulties that were identified by Casey?

In Activity 8.1 some of the difficulties which Casey might have to overcome were identified. In this section the difficulties are revisited with some suggestions on how Casey could have applied theory to help resolve them.

Single level of qualification but students with very different entry levels

Achievement is a powerful motivator for students; however, humanists argue that the only valuable form of assessment is self-assessment where individuals identify personal growth. Initially dividing students into engineered groups or allowing students to self-select groups on the basis of their existing knowledge and understanding will allow them to feel safe as they will be working with peers they perceive to be operating at a similar level. Within the group, students will be able to assess or reassess their knowledge and understanding and interact with others in order to identify and rectify areas of weakness while supporting the learning of others.

Students with variable experience and expectations of teaching and learning

By using a variety of different activities and teaching methods, the teacher will be able to meet students' different experiences and expectations of teaching and learning. As the group develops, the teacher will be able to identify which methods work best in terms of teaching and learning and utilise these to best effect within their planning.

Some students needing additional support due to behavioural issues, some with literacy issues, others with limited attentions spans, and so on

Working together in collaboration with peers in small groups can provide an informal mechanism for students with some support needs. Students with literacy issues can be supported through the use of different media, for example researching using computers which offer screen readers or the use of coloured backgrounds instead of using books. Providing information to all students in the form of concise, bullet-pointed handouts or exercises can also help students to feel included in the learning process. Differentiated tasks with achievable outcomes can help less confident students to feel included in the learning process. Tasks with a limited amount of time for completion help students to focus on the expected outcome. Using a series of short, related tasks which enable students to progress towards an identified outcome, rather than a single task, can also help retain student focus.

Students previously identified by other staff as being 'lazy'

It is always possible that 'laziness' may be hiding an unidentified learning need. It is equally possible that the student finds the work either too difficult or too easy or it could simply be that the student is either bored or has no interest in the subject. Whatever the case it usually takes the teacher little time to discover the reason for the cause of the perceived 'laziness'. In the introduction it was mentioned that Casey had been asked to take on a pastoral role for a group of students, and in the capacity of a mentor Casey may be able to discover the root cause of the laziness and take the appropriate action (see Chapter 4).

Noisy students who do not give the teacher their attention

By providing differentiated but related group-based tasks to students Casey could encourage students to play to their strength and continue talking, but to be talking with a purpose. Fast-moving interactive tasks with specific outcomes will allow interaction and can help students to remain focussed on the tasks in hand.

Chapter summary

A long time ago I was taught that anything a teacher does in a classroom can be connected to a theory – all the teacher had to do was work out which one, why it worked and how to use it again.

In this chapter we have looked at what is meant by 'mixing it up' in terms of using parts of different theories or schools of theory to devise strategies which will meet the needs of students and enable them to learn effectively and efficiently.

MENTOR MOMENT

Mixing it up in terms of applying theory in teaching is something that most teachers will do unconsciously rather than making a conscious effort to include different theories within their professional practice. Linking theory to our practice is not something we spend a lot of time considering but an understanding of different theories and how they can be applied in practice can help us to overcome or ameliorate problems. Generally, a mixed approach in terms of the application of theory in teaching and learning is something that can enhance both processes and it is well worth spending some time thinking about how you use different theories in your professional practice. Think about the following questions and discuss them with your mentor at your next meeting.

- What theories do I use in my teaching?
- Do you think that theories can be more appropriate to some groups rather than others and why do you think this is?
- What steps could you take to try different theoretical approaches in your professional practice?
- What do you think the benefits of using mixed theories would be for you and your students?
- How do you think your students would react to being taught in this way?

Suggested further reading

Belbin, M (2004) *Management Teams: Why They Succeed or Fail* (2nd ed). Oxford: Elsevier Butterworth-Heinemann.

Berne, E (1961) *Transactional Analysis in Psychotherapy: A Systematic Individual and Social Psychiatry*. New York: Grove Press.

References

Ausubel, DP (1960) The use of advance organizers in the learning and retention of meaningful verbal material. *Journal of Educational Psychology*, 51: 267–72.

Bandura, A (1977) *Social Learning Theory*. New York: General Learning Press.

Becker, H (1973) [1963] *Outsiders*. New York: Free Press.

Belbin, M (2004) *Management Teams: Why They Succeed or Fail* (2nd ed). Oxford: Elsevier Butterworth-Heinemann.

Berne, **E** (1961) *Transactional Analysis in Psychotherapy: A Systematic Individual and Social Psychiatry*. New York: Grove Press.

Bloom, **B**, **Englehart**, **MD**, **Furst**, **E**, **Hill**, **W and Krathwohl**, **D** (1956) *Taxonomy of Educational Objectives: The Classification of Educational Goals. Handbook I: Cognitive Domain*. New York, Toronto: Longmans, Green.

Bruner, **JS** (1960) *The Process of Education*. Cambridge, MA: Harvard University Press.

Candy, **PC** (1991) *Self-Direction for Lifelong Learning*. San Francisco, CA: Jossey-Bass.

Dyson, **A** (2001) Special needs in the twenty-first century: where we've been and where we're going. *British Journal of Special Education*, 28 (1): 24–8.

Goffman, **E** (1963) *Stigma: Notes on the Management of Spoiled Identity*. Englewood Cliffs, NY: Prentice Hall.

Knowles, **MS**, **Holton**, **EF and Swanson**, **RA** (2015) *The Adult Learner* (8th ed). Abingdon: Routledge.

Korthagen, **FAJ and Kessels**, **JPA** (1999) Linking theory and practice: changing the pedagogy of teacher education. *Educational Researcher*, 28 (4): 4–17.

Maslow, **AH** (1943) A theory of human motivation. *Psychological Review*, 50 (4): 370–96.

Mills, **D and Alexander**, **P** (2013) *Small Group Teaching: A Toolkit for Learning*. York: Higher Education Academy.

Piaget, **J** (1936) *Origins of Intelligence in the Child*. London: Routledge and Kegan Paul.

Rogers, **C** (1959) A theory of therapy, personality and interpersonal relationships as developed in the client-centered framework, in Koch, S (ed) *Psychology: A Study of a Science. Volume 3: Formulations of the Person and the Social Context*. New York: McGraw Hill.

Schön, **DA** (1991) *The Reflective Practitioner: How Professionals Think in Action*. Abingdon: Routledge.

Tuckman, **BW** (1965) Developmental sequence in small groups. *Psychological Bulletin*, 63 (6): 384–99.

Vygotsky, **LS** (1978) *Mind in Society: The Development of Higher Psychological Processes*. Cambridge, MA: Harvard University Press.

9

INNOVATIVE TEACHING

In this chapter we will explore:

• defining innovation in teaching;

• using reflection to improve your teaching;

• creativity and creative teaching strategies.

Introduction

It is quite usual to assume that the success of any education system is dependent upon the quality of its teachers. Teachers are responsible for preparing the young for life and work and the not-so-young for a whole range of activities and life events. Education permeates our existence at so many important stages and, as such, has the power to both advance and inhibit thinking. It is little wonder that we strive for innovative teaching practice which engages students and supports learning.

Most teachers are introduced to various forms of pedagogy which encompass a range of approaches to teaching and some will have in-depth knowledge of theory which provides them with a framework for understanding how people learn. As a result, these teachers should be able to make informed decisions about how best to teach, yet many will still base their teaching approach on what worked for them as learners and others will be restricted by the teaching guidelines informed by their employing organisations. The overall outcome of this is that teaching becomes far more uniform and less innovative than we would like.

When we talk about innovative practice we may make reference to classroom strategies or the use of interesting resources. This often includes technology or specific 'toolkits' which teachers can employ to plan interesting lessons. There are many documented examples we can refer to and a plethora of online guides to help us, but very few of these take account of the fact that every teaching and learning situation is unique and as such teachers need to learn how to adapt, rather than replicate successful approaches.

In this chapter we are introduced to Samir, an enthusiastic young teacher who has recently finished training. Samir is passionate about creating engaging lessons and is very keen to experiment with new strategies and learning resources.

Figure 9.1 Samir's story

---- CASE STUDY ----

Samir's journal

My first real job! I can't believe how lucky I have been, I feel like the job was just made for me. I absolutely loved my training and learned so much about approaches to teaching. It was great having a supportive mentor who encouraged me to try out new things and guided me without actually telling me what to do. So now I just can't wait to get started ... my head is buzzing with ideas.

Defining innovation in teaching

As with many things, 'innovative teaching' is not that easy to define. It could refer to teaching that is context based, involves learning through doing, includes the integration of new ideas or is in some way ahead of its time. The word innovation relates to something which is advanced and forward-looking, so often includes ideas which are fresh and unusual. This would suggest that innovative teaching methods fall into the camp of proactive, rather than reactive, approaches. There is a misconception that innovation in teaching simply refers to the generation of new ideas which suggests it might be accessible to just a few creative individuals ... but is this the case, or can we innovate through a range of strategies and a shared approach to planning and developing learning?

There are a number of factors which relate to innovation in teaching and the following list may provide a starting point for developing your own ideas.

- Remove the pressure to produce the right answers.

- Value risk-taking.

- Make learning engaging and fun.

- Encourage interaction and challenge.

- Promote learners' creativity.

Value risk-taking by removing the pressure to produce the right answers

Innovative teaching is often linked to constructivist and student-centred approaches, whereby students are encouraged to be active participants engaged in problem-solving activities. Its focus is on creating an environment which is conducive to learning and in which students feel supported enough to take risks, i.e. they are not always seeking to produce the 'right' answer but are focussed on extending their learning. This means creating an environment in which questions are encouraged, and are responded to appropriately, where not getting the right answer is seen as an opportunity to explore a topic further and where a lesson plan is simply a rough guide for the lesson, not a template to be slavishly followed.

Make learning engaging and fun

Another important aspect of innovative teaching is creating engaging lessons which make learning enjoyable and memorable. This may simply involve changing the structure of the lesson, reorganising the classroom, using a range of resources or including fun activities. The important thing is that a learning environment should not be too predictable – do we always need to start a lesson with learning objectives? Is it necessary to *always* have a starter activity? Do we need to follow a formulaic approach to planning to ensure that we have all the key elements outlined in what might be defined by your organisation as an 'outstanding' lesson? Students do become used to lesson structure very quickly; this has its benefits in that it provides the comfort and safety of what is known and predictable, however, it also provides an opportunity to 'switch off'. I once taught a lesson to adult learners where my introduction to the lesson was *we do not have any learning objectives*; I then preceded to tell them that they were going to lead the lesson by sharing some of their experiences. This was a contradiction to the very safe structure I had previously provided and immediately focussed their attention as they were unsure about what would happen next. When someone arrived late, the update that was provided by one of his peers was, *we are not having any objectives* ... clearly this one action had a dramatic impact on how they viewed the lesson. The safety net of the previous structure had been removed and they now had to focus on what happened next. This was one of the most productive lessons we had; the students may have felt some initial discomfort at the change in approach but they were focussed throughout.

That particular lesson did make me reflect on how we often have standard approaches to planning our teaching and how this can also limit learning. It also made me question the benefit of sharing learning objectives (something I rarely do now). That is not to say that I don't share the intent and purpose of the learning or make links to what we have learned in the past; it simply means I don't start the lesson by reading out and (perhaps worse) encouraging people to write down a list of rather meaningless statements. That, of course, is personal opinion, I am sure some teachers find innovative ways of working with learning objectives – and if that is the case, I would certainly encourage them to share those ideas.

CASE STUDY

Samir's journal

I have been really trying to create a positive classroom environment and it seems to be working. My students certainly aren't afraid of asking questions or of contributing to discussion. There is a real buzz in the room and they seem to be enjoying taking part in the activities I have set for them. There is only one slight issue ... when I decided to give them more freedom to choose activities, they actually got very excited about it, which was great. But in their excitement they were talking and talking. Three different groups babbling away and the noise level in the classroom rising higher and higher. I noticed the Head of Department peering through the window with a slightly disapproving look on her face and wondered if I should try to calm them down ... the only thing is, they were just excited about the task; it seems churlish to squash that enthusiasm!

Encourage interaction and challenge

There is evidence to suggest that student interaction has a positive effect on learning (Gillies et al., 2008) and much of this is discussed in Chapter 6. Co-operative learning encourages the development of prosocial behaviours as well as higher-level thinking skills and helps to create an environment in which learners are able to problem-solve and construct their own meaning of new concepts. However, it isn't enough to simply include group work in the hope that this will inspire innovation. Group activities must be purposeful and include the right amount of challenge if they are to help students to reach their full potential. In this sense, the innovative teacher will know how to scaffold activities to ensure that every student is able to participate, will intervene when focus is drifting off-task and will know when to step back to allow learning to take place. It is a difficult balance and one which requires the development of honest reflection on your own actions.

One important consideration in relation to the introduction of interaction and challenge is the impact of emotional state on our thinking. Generally, students learn more effectively when they feel secure, happy and excited about what they are doing (Boekaerts, 1993), but emotions can also have a negative effect. If students are overly excited or enthusiastic they might work too quickly or carelessly and, in my experience, over-excited learners are often very noisy which can impact on individuals within the class. This seems to be the case in Samir's class too and it is important to develop strategies to channel excitement in ways which mean that all learners can feel heard. One possible strategy is to organise group rules for the activity; this provides the option to recognise and reward enthusiasm for the task at the same time as getting students to acknowledge that noise levels can rise in confined spaces and can also be disruptive to learning.

Promote learners' creativity

Innovative teaching, by its very nature, should at the same time promote innovation within learning. Therefore, a definition of innovative teaching should also include the stimulation of learners' creative potential. This idea is linked to the notion of progression and individual development, concepts which are firmly embedded into our beliefs about learning. Learning itself can be viewed as growth; it has its roots planted in the foundations of knowledge but is also viewed as a journey – we very rarely hop from not knowing something to instantly knowing as there is usually a process of accommodating new information. Gustav Klimt's famous painting, *The Tree of Life*, depicts this journey through an abundance of twists and turns representing life's often circuitous route, and the tree reaches towards the sky which is said to represent man's eternal quest to be more than he currently is (**Gustav Klimt.com,** online).

The promotion of learners' creativity is not only an attractive idea, it is probably essential if we are to prepare people for the modern workplace. Therefore, finding ways of encouraging this within the classroom is a crucial aspect of innovative teaching. According to Epstein and Phan (2012), there are four key competencies which help to build creativity; these are:

1.   capturing new ideas;

2.   challenging – giving ourselves difficult problems to solve;

3.   broadening – boosting creativity by learning new and interesting things;

4.   surrounding – associating with interesting and diverse things and people.

Figure 9.2 A tree of life

Of these, the most important is considered to be the capturing of ideas, which is something that should be encouraged on a daily basis. Within a learning environment this could be done in a number of ways, including the use of personal scrapbooks, journals or ideas boxes. These needn't be arduous tasks but should become an integrated part of classroom practice. The capturing of ideas in this way is also a way of validating them. By recognising the importance of ideas we are at the same time giving students permission to have them.

It is also important that teachers model creativity in their own teaching. By taking imaginative approaches to teaching and taking risks in the strategies we adopt we are also modelling the ways in which creativity can enhance learning. At the same time we may be demonstrating that when things don't go according to plan this is not something to fear but an opportunity to learn something new. Epstein and Phan (2012) also suggest that teachers dedicate five minutes a day to creative training activities such as problem-solving or idea-generation activities.

ACTIVITY 9.1

Put together a list of creative teaching activities you could incorporate into your lessons. These could be any activities that encourage people to come up with solutions to a problem, generate 'out-of-the-box' ideas or simply stretch the boundaries of thinking. Try to come up with at least 20 things and don't censure your ideas. When you have your list, arrange to talk it through with a colleague or your mentor ... you never know what might come of that discussion.

Diffusion of innovation

As stated at the beginning of this chapter, the ability to be innovative is not the preserve of a fortunate few but is something we can all aspire to. This is supported by Roger's diffusion of innovation theory (2003) which suggests that innovative teaching is not necessarily about creating entirely new approaches but may be about using strategies or resources in more innovative ways.

Diffusion of innovation describes how, over a period of time, an idea gains momentum and spreads through the social system, the end result being that people adopt the new idea and make it their own. Adoption simply means that the idea, or resource, is adapted by the other person and some aspect of it becomes different. This can be viewed as a form of innovation that did not require the generation of an entirely original idea.

We could even argue that 'truly original' ideas are probably something of a myth as the vast majority of innovations seem to be an adaptation of something that we are already familiar with. In Leonardo Da Vinci's drawings, studies of bird flight inspired the initial ideas about human flight, and more recently the Japanese bullet trains were inspired by the kingfisher. The trains originally burdened by sonic boom caused by changing air pressure were redesigned when engineers noticed that kingfishers travel between air and water with minimal splash. The trains were remodelled with a long beak-shaped nose which significantly reduced the amount of noise they made and allowed them to travel 10 per cent faster. These are indeed innovative ideas ... but are they truly original, or adaptations of the natural world?

Using reflection to improve your teaching

Reflective practice involves a process of learning from experiences in ways which develop new insights about ourselves and how we work. Through meaningful reflection we are able to develop greater self-awareness and critically examine our thoughts, feelings and actions. The purpose is to recapture experiences and think about them objectively in order to gain new understandings. In teaching, this is a very important activity, so long as it is done with honesty and integrity. Reflective practice should always be focussed on what we can learn; it is not a process of justifying our actions.

Models of reflection

Reflection can involve any activity which causes us to think about experiences in a way which provokes questions about our actions. It could be as simple as keeping a journal of thoughts and ideas but, for some people, reflection is more effective if it is more formally structured. There are a number of reflective models you could adopt to do this and it is worth spending some time thinking about the best approach for you if this is to become a useful activity. A popular model is that produced by Gibbs (1988) which includes six stages as shown in Figure 9.3.

Figure 9.3 Gibbs' Model of Reflection

This model is described as an iterative model, which means learning through repetition and, because of this, the cycle element is important. It is not simply a case of recording an experience but also involves thinking about how that experience might be altered by taking a different approach or generating a new understanding.

According to Bolton (2001), reflective practice is enhanced by becoming reflexively aware. This means considering your own thoughts in relation to a particular incident and can be done by developing a mindful approach and giving careful consideration to the complexity of situations, rather than simply recording objective observations. Bolton suggests using a *through the looking glass* model which is based on three foundations.

1. Certain uncertainty.

2. Serious playfulness.

3. Unquestioning questioning.

This model can be a little uncomfortable for some people as it removes the aspect of 'knowing' something. In the Gibbs model you are asked to describe what happened, so you assess a situation, then make an evaluation, analyse this and come to some conclusions about the best action to take. You are, in effect, encouraged to make decisions all the way through the process, thereby providing some sense of security that you are 'in control' of the situation. By taking a *through the looking glass* approach we are not looking for simple answers but are accepting the notion of *certain uncertainty*, which recognises that the only thing which is really certain is that we can never have certainty. Acceptance of this point negates notions of knowing the answer at any given time, something which can be difficult when we are reflecting in order to seek specific solutions to issues or concerns. Bolton argues that the only way to make sense of this is by adopting *serious playfulness* which means being willing to try out a range of things rather than seeking a specific answer. Within this, *unquestioning questioning* provides an opportunity to generate new meaning and abandon previously held 'truths'. In a way, this is about developing our curiosity so that we become open to new ideas and possibilities, like Alice in her amazing adventures; being curiouser and curiouser we are adding a new dimension to our learning.

Developing reflexivity does require a little practice and the following questions may be a useful starting point.

*   What do I think and feel about this?

*   What assumptions am I making?

*   In what ways does my experience influence my reflections?

*   How do these things influence my choices and actions?

Using reflection to enhance understanding can be liberating and very helpful in developing professional competence, but it should be acknowledged that the process can also be unsettling and can have an intense emotional impact. Brookfield likens it to laying down psychological dynamite: *Questioning the assumptions on which we act and exploring alternative ideas are not only difficult but also psychologically explosive* ... (Brookfield, 1990, p178).

The purpose of reflection is to strive for constant improvement, which is certainly a positive thing but also contains the potential danger of self-flagellation. Therefore, it is imperative to remember the key principle of objectivity and noting that criticality, in the form of purposeful thinking, does not necessarily mean criticising. It is important that reflective practice has a genuine purpose and is contextualised within the professional role. This allows us to be more objective and avoids the temptation for it to become of form of egocentric navel-gazing.

CASE STUDY

Samir's journal

So ... I had a chat with my mentor who had some ideas about harnessing my students' energy in positive ways and eventually I decided to set some 'rules for group work'. This did work ... they now effectively 'police' their own activities. They get on with the work I have set them and they keep each other in check so the classroom doesn't ever really get noisy. In some ways this is perfect. But something is bothering me ... and I just don't know what it is? The group seems to have lost something. I think it is to do with the excitement they had when I first started teaching them. They used to ask lots of questions and seemed to be buzzing with ideas. Now they just seem to be compliant. This is frustrating ... I fear I will never get it right.

Samir's frustration is tangible. It seems he had found a solution to his initial problem and by implementing something to deal with that problem he seems to have created another issue. One of the things that may be causing this is that Samir was too eager to resolve his first teaching issue and didn't really think through his approach. His reflection went through a typical cycle of recording and analysing a situation and then he immediately sought a solution. If Samir had taken a more reflexive approach he may have considered the underlying assumptions informing his decisions which could well have led to a change of priority. Samir was concerned that the Head of Department had seen how noisy his class was and he immediately took this as a sign that something was wrong. Was he assuming that the Head of Department had more knowledge about teaching than him? Is someone in authority a better judge of what should or should not be happening in the classroom? By taking a more reflexive approach, Samir would have thought about his own response to this and would have questioned his attitude to teaching or perhaps to authority. He would have thought about his own values and the assumptions he was making as a result. Reflexivity expands our frame of reference and encourages us to become aware of our own limitations and how these influence our actions.

In an action-focussed model of reflection it is possible that you may implement corrective actions before you are clear about why a particular event occurred and, in doing so, could miss some important information. By taking a *through the looking glass* approach we are not looking for simple answers but are accepting the notion of *certain uncertainty*. Acceptance of this point negates the need to know the answer or find a solution to a problem and it also means releasing a little bit of control. Both are useful; it is simply about choosing the right approach for the individual and the situation. In Samir's case, taking a reflexive approach would have meant that he tested ideas which may have gone against his initial assumptions about teaching and learning; for example, encouraging students to talk and go off-task or removing teacher control from group activities. Samir clearly had some assumptions about what a positive classroom would look like ... what if he was wrong about that – would his approach have been different?

This type of reflection can be very powerful in generating a range of options, which in turn can transform our practice as long as we are able to approach the process with openness and honesty.

CASE STUDY

Samir's journal

I have spent a lot of time reflecting on how I manage my groups, have chatted to my mentor, and had a word with the Head of Department after she spotted my rather noisy group. It turns out she was impressed by the level of activity and not at all worried about the noise level; she said she trusted that 'I had that under control' ... not sure I really did at that point but it was nice to know I was trusted. So what does this all mean? Actually one thing I have learned is to trust my own judgement a bit more. I think because I am new to the job I just assumed that other people knew more than me .... They probably do about lots of things but they aren't actually in my class and really they only know what I tell them about my teaching. I want my students to be actively involved in their learning but I want them to listen to me when they need to ... so last week we discussed a signal I could use when the noise levels were getting too much. We agreed on waving as this meant that everyone could see the signal easily ... and guess what? It worked! Better than that, sometimes the students do it themselves.

It is strange but now I am not at all worried about a slightly noisy class; I just want to make sure they get the most out of each lesson and I definitely want to think of interesting ways of teaching my subject and I have spent a lot of time exploring different strategies that I can adapt for my class.

Creativity and creative teaching strategies

Picasso is attributed with the quote *all children are artists, the problem is staying an artist when you grow up* (Pablo Picasso Quotes online, 2018). This sentiment aligns to Sir Ken Robinson's key message in the RSA Animate Changing Education Paradigms (RSA, 2010) in which education is defined as a system that has been modelled on industrialisation, with roots firmly embedded in standardised practice. If this is the case, how do we encourage teachers to be creative as well as build fertile ground for creativity within classrooms?

The word 'creative' conjures up images of ethereal worlds surrounded by magical events. It is often associated with artistic endeavour and similarly artistic people. These are the 'special few' who have a mysterious ability that the rest of us can only dream about. But, according to Robinson (2017) this is a misconception. If we take creativity in its broadest context then it should also include the day-to-day activities which might be carried out by less than magical people in every ordinary workplace. Robinson stresses that in order to progress as a society we need to recognise wider creativities and learn to think differently about talents and abilities. His main assertion is that every one of us has the ability to be creative and that our challenge as a society is to generate a culture in which innovation is something we can all be involved in. This view is reinforced by Edwards (2001) who suggests that current systems of education may neglect important aspects of creativity by focussing on the scientific and treating the arts as 'enrichment'. This, in turn, reduces the importance of valuable human capabilities which have the potential to lead change, such as perception, intuition and imagination. Perhaps this is a reaction to the perceived need to control education processes by having a focus on rationality, particularly when we view education as a vehicle for workplace preparation. This is not an illogical approach, but as Samples (1976) suggests, it may also be inhibiting progress and, making reference to Einstein, he states that by ignoring that which is not considered rational, we may be limiting our potential:

Einstein called the intuitive or metaphoric mind a sacred gift. He added that the rational mind was a faithful servant. It is paradoxical that in the context of modern life we have begun to worship the servant and defile the divine.

(1976, p26)

Creative teaching strategies

Robinson (2017) suggests that creativity has three key components: imagination, which brings to mind ideas; creativity, described as the process through which we develop original ideas; and innovation, whereby we put new ideas into practice. In the classic work, *The Act of Creation* (1964), Koestler introduced the term *bisociation* which refers to the combination of an object or idea from two fields that are not normally considered to be related. By combining these two objects or ideas we merge them in a new way and create something different. An example of this is adapted for the teaching context in Kung Fu punctuation, whereby punctuation is taught through the use of Kung Fu moves (**www.youtube.com/watch?v=Q35SfhGCL8Q&t=3s**).

It is a difficult task to provide guidance on creative teaching strategies as by doing so we immediately remove some of their unique attributes. For me, creativity is defined as *adapting aspects of thought, knowledge or nature in unique ways.* If I simply produce a list of creative teaching strategies to be followed they lose the benefit of adaptation and uniqueness and immediately become less creative. It is a dilemma, so I have conveyed my own ideas in the form of a mind map, followed by a discussion on some strategies which might be considered 'creative' but which I would recommend you adapt, rather than adopt.

Figure 9.4 Creative teaching mind map

When trainee teachers were asked what it meant to be creative, they defined the process as:

- thinking outside the box;

- problem-solving;

- doing things differently;

- taking risks;

- artistic – using music, drawing, painting;

- opening up minds, exploring.

(Eastwood et al., 2009, p2)

These are all things which could be adapted for classroom practice.

Using case studies and problem-solving activities encourages students to 'think outside of the box' although they do usually include some boundaries in the form of the study used. An alternative, and probably more challenging activity, would be to outline a scenario and ask students to create a case study or story around this. This gives them more control over the activity and is certainly more challenging than solving a given problem. In fact, they are very likely to highlight problems you hadn't even thought about.

Doing things differently could relate to a number of aspects of teaching. This could simply involve changing the structure of the lesson, including elements of surprise in activities or tapping into a range of senses, for example using music, colour or sense of smell within the classroom.

The idea of taking risks can be met with some scepticism. We live in a litigious society and any sort of professional risk is generally frowned upon; add to that very strict guidelines in relation to health and safety, emotional well-being and the 'fragility' of learners and the likelihood of risk-taking in the classroom becomes less and less. But what do we actually mean by taking a risk in teaching? In life this usually refers to trying something which may go wrong; we take a risk when we do things differently, when we make ourselves vulnerable, when there is a chance we may be rejected or that we may not 'be good enough' – all of these things present emotional, social and, sometimes, financial risks. In the classroom, risk-taking is much the same; it is when we try something that may not work, when we adopt a different approach, when we use a strategy that is not tried and tested, when we provide students with the opportunity to question our actions, abilities or even knowledge. We can take risks when we lessen our control, when we learn with our students, when we let them teach or let a lesson go off-plan. Taking a risk in teaching can be likened to taking a risk in life; it involves daring to see things differently and treating teaching as an indefinite adventure rather than a highly prescribed activity. As Helen Keller famously said, *life is either a daring adventure or nothing* (Keller, 1946, pp50–1).

Taking an 'artistic' approach to teaching may involve using activities such as creating music, drawing or painting. The type of strategy adopted very much depends on the students and having some knowledge of their abilities, skills, likes and dislikes. Often students (and teachers) will say that they cannot draw or paint and may be thrown into a panic if they are asked to do this in the classroom, so consider alternatives such as mind maps or collage. Artistic approaches are really about using a wider range of senses and applying learning in different ways. This can be achieved by:

- creating drawings;

- making posters or mind maps;

- writing songs or poems;

- making models out of play-dough;

- creating things out of a range of random objects.

These strategies can be used in any subject and can provide a really good platform for discussion. I have used the play-dough approach when getting students to describe learning theories. The students were asked to create a model which represented their understanding of the theory and then make a short video in which they described the model. This involved a range of skills and also meant that the theory had to be discussed and understood before the model could be created.

Opening up minds and exploring new ideas is a fundamental part of any lesson as without this all we are doing is delivering content, probably for the purpose of passing assessments. All of the strategies we have discussed in this chapter have the potential to open minds. Any form of discussion, any practical experience or activity will provide a prompt for thinking which in turn opens the door to new ideas. Innovative teaching most certainly requires an approach which allows learners to construct new meanings and sees learning as a process of exploration. While there is no one strategy for opening our minds, it could be argued that anything which challenges our thinking is a good starting point. Here are five ideas to get you started.

1. *Scripted fantasy* – this is based on a technique employed in teaching social and emotional skills and the use of a short relaxation exercise followed by a series of suggestions which form a framework of the 'fantasy'. The participants are then free to enter the world of their own imagination, taking the fantasy to wherever they see fit (Hall and Leech, 1990).

2. *Picture association* – imagery is often linked to our creative capacities as it allows us to both view and depict things in non-linear ways. Using images to prompt or to generate ideas is a useful way to start discussion.

3. *Using 'thinking hats'* – this technique is based on the work of Edward de Bono (2000) and is used as a strategy for generating solutions to problems. The thinking hats provide a platform to explore issues from different perspectives which force people to move away from their preferred thinking style. The hats each have a different colour and purpose, for example:

    - the white hat considers the 'facts';

    - the yellow hat symbolises optimism and focusses on the positives;

    - the black hat represents judgement – it could be the devil's advocate, it spots dangers and difficulties;

    - the red hat signifies feelings – when 'wearing' this hat you can express emotions such as likes, fears, dislikes, love, hate;

- the green hat has a focus on creativity and seeks out possibilities and new ideas;

- the blue hat manages the thinking process – it keeps the others under control and ensures that guidelines are followed.

4. *Sand-box* – Sand-box activities allow a person to construct his or her own microcosm using miniature objects such as people, animals, trees, houses, etc. and a tray full of sand (Dale and Lyddon, 1998). With these a scene is created which can form the basis of discussion or idea generation.

5. *Telling stories* – I am a great believer in stories and often use them to start or end a class. I think there is something quite therapeutic about someone reading to you and perhaps this allows us to relax and start to think about new ideas. Short stories or poems which include an important message or open up a general discussion are the best as they contain just enough information to prompt questions.

PAUSE POINT

Which of these ideas appeal to you? What is good or not so good about them? How might you adapt them for your teaching?

Chapter summary

In this chapter we have explored the meaning of innovative teaching and thought about ways you can use different approaches to improve classroom practice. We have also considered the importance of reflecting honestly on what you currently do in order to discover new approaches you could try.

MENTOR MOMENT

In this section we have included starter points for discussions with mentors so that you can talk through the chapter content. The aim of the questions is to encourage you to interrogate your understanding of the concepts presented and consider ways in which these might influence your teaching.

- What does creative teaching 'look like' to you?
- What types of things could you try?
- What might be the potential obstacles?
- In what ways could you work with others to overcome any obstacles?

Suggested further reading

Bolton, G (2001) *Reflective Practice, Writing and Professional Development*. London: Paul Chapman Publishing Ltd.

Robinson, K (2017) *Out of Our Minds: The Power of Being Creative* (3rd ed). Oxford: John Wiley and Sons Ltd.

References

Boekaerts, M (1993) Being concerned with well-being and with learning. *Educational Psychologist*, 28 (2): 149–67.

Bolton, G (2001) *Reflective Practice, Writing and Professional Development*. London: Paul Chapman Publishing Ltd.

Brookfield, SD (1990) Using critical incidents to explore learners' assumptions, in Mezirow, J (ed) *Fostering Critical Reflection in Adulthood*. San Francisco, CA: Jossey-Bass.

Dale, MA and Lyddon, WJ (1998) Sandplay: a constructivist strategy for assessment and change. *Journal of Constructivist Psychology*, 13 (2): 135–54.

De Bono, E (2000) *Six Thinking Hats*. London: Penguin.

Eastwood, L, Coates, J, Dixon, L, Harvey, J, Ormondroyd, C and Williamson, S (2009) *A Toolkit for Creative Teaching in Post-Compulsory Education*. Maidenhead: Open University Press, McGraw-Hill.

Edwards, B (2001) *The New Drawing on the Right Side of the Brain*. London: HarperCollins.

Epstein, R and Phan, V (2012) Which competencies are most important for creative expression? *Creativity Research Journal*, 24 (4): 278–82.

Gibbs, G (1988) *Learning by Doing: A Guide to Teaching and Learning*. London: FEU.

Gillies, RM, Ashman, AF and Terwell, J (2008) *The Teacher's Role in Implementing Co-operative Learning in the Classroom*. New York: Springer.

Hall, E and Leech, A (1990) *Fantasy in the Classroom*. London: Routledge.

Keller, H (1946) Faith fears not, in *Let Us Have Faith*. New York: Doubleday.

Koestler, A (1964) *The Act of Creation*. London: Hutchinson and Co, Longman.

Kung Fu punctuation Available at **www.youtube.com/watch?v=Q35SfhGCL8Q&t=3s** (Accessed 24 March 2019).

Robinson, K (2017) *Out of Our Minds: The Power of Being Creative* (3rd ed). Oxford: John Wiley and Sons Ltd.

Rogers, **EM** (2003) *Diffusion of Innovations* (5th ed). New York: Free Press.

RSA (2010) RSA Animate: changing education paradigms. Available at **www.youtube.com/watch?v=zDZFcDGpL4U**

Samples, **B** (1976) *The Metaphoric Mind: A Celebration of Creative Consciousness.* Boston, MA: Addison-Wesley Publishing Company.

10

RESILIENCE

In this chapter we will explore:

- psychological resilience;
- strategies for developing resilience.

Introduction

Most of us experience times when we find it more difficult to cope with day-to-day life, especially if we are working in demanding jobs. Teaching certainly fits this category, indeed it has been recognised as one of the most challenging occupations in terms of work-related anxiety and stress (Health and Safety Executive, 2018) so considering ways in which we can manage stress and build our resilience is an essential part of the role.

When faced with difficulties, someone who has developed resilience is more likely to be able to 'bounce back' from set-backs. This has several advantages, not least of these is the way in which it helps to build confidence overall. If we believe we can recover from difficult situations, we have more faith in our ability to handle challenges. Highly resilient people, therefore, are more able to adapt to different circumstances and find positive ways of moving forwards.

In this chapter we are introduced to Rachel, an NQT (Newly Qualified Teacher) who feels she 'struggled' through her teacher training and was lucky to get a job at the end of it.

Psychological resilience

Psychological resilience is a term used to describe a person's capacity to withstand stress without damaging consequences such as negative mood or mental illness. It could also be described as an individual's ability to thrive despite the presence of stressors. This means that, in some cases, resilient people will not only survive stressful situations but will be able to experience them as challenges from which they can learn and develop.

Figure 10.1 Rachel's story

According to cognitive psychologists, our ability to manage difficult situations effectively is linked to our perceptions of the world, themselves developed through how we have learned to think about things. Lakoff and Johnson (2003) suggest that our thoughts are not only linked to cognitive ability but also have an impact on how we perceive life and, in turn, how we relate to others and the world around us. These norms of thinking influence every aspect of our lives and often become apparent in tendencies towards an optimistic or pessimistic approach, something which most people assume is a personality trait. Seligman (2018), however, suggests that optimism is something which can be learned, allowing us to develop the ability to view things from a positive perspective.

Learned optimism

Seligman's research (originally focussed on learned helplessness) led to a model of 'learned optimism'. In Seligman's view, we each have an 'attributional style' which describes how we explain life events to ourselves. It is suggested that such explanations have three elements, referred to as the three Ps; these are:

1. *personalisation* – concerned with whether we view a particular outcome as being due to internal or external factors. Was the success or failure of something due to our inherent abilities/inabilities or was it caused by external conditions?;

2. *permanence* – relates to the degree to which we might view an outcome as temporary or permanent. Someone with a pessimistic outlook might view a positive outcome as a 'one-off' or a negative event as being permanently fixed. In contrast, optimists would view success as a permanent factor, which they may attribute to some inherent ability and will see negative outcomes as being transient;

3. *Pervasiveness* – explains an individual's view on the globality or specificity of events, i.e. if we have a tendency to consider things to be consistent and widespread, rather than more specific or contextual. We might have experienced some bad luck and assume that we are unlucky (therefore, will continue to have bad luck) or we may link this to a specific set of criteria and accept that this was a single event rather than a life script.

CASE STUDY

Rachel's journal

I can't believe I actually got this job. My interview didn't go at all well – I went over on the micro-teach by three minutes and I am sure I just mumbled my answers to the questions. Never mind, by some sort of fluke I am here. The first few weeks have gone well – I suspect that is because I am lucky enough to have good students, but tomorrow I am being observed by the Head of Department. I am panicking! Now they will see the real me ... I just hope the students don't play up!

Rachel seems to have personalised her experience by accrediting her success to external factors such as luck or having good students. She has not recognised her own part in making a success of both her job interview and her teaching to date. In addition, she seems to be showing some signs of 'imposter syndrome', a pattern of doubting her abilities which ultimately leads to a fear of being exposed as a 'fraud' (Clance and Imes, 1978). This has led to a certain dread about being observed by the Head of Department, something which viewed in a different way could actually be a very positive experience and a chance to show what she is capable of.

Locus of control

Locus of control describes the way in which we view our responses to events. According to Buchanen and Seligman (1995), this can be categorised as internal or external depending on how we view things. People with an internal locus of control tend to believe that events are a direct response to their characteristics and how they manage things, whereas those with an external locus of control regard outcomes as being largely independent of them and therefore out of their control. This is evident in the way Rachel thinks about her students, hoping that they will behave when the Head of Department visits her lesson. This suggests that she feels this variable is completely outside of her control and immediately makes her more vulnerable in this particular situation.

Locus of control is associated with how we attribute success and failure which, in turn, has an impact on how motivated we might be to ensure our success in a particular endeavour. If someone expects to succeed and sees that success as something over which they have some control, they are more likely to be motivated and seek out strategies which will help them to achieve their desired outcomes. Conversely, if we attribute our success or failure to luck or fate, it is more difficult to find the motivation required to focus our efforts effectively; we are also more likely to experience stress or anxiety as we feel we have less general control over our lives. Research suggests that people with an internal locus of control have higher self-esteem and more effective coping strategies (Macsinga and Nemeti, 2012).

Self-efficacy

Another important aspect relating to how we might approach challenges is our belief in our capability. Bandura referred to this as self-efficacy, which he described as our belief that we have the ability to influence the events of our lives (2008). Self-efficacy shapes how we think and feel about things and, as a result, has an impact on our motivations and behaviours, so those people with high self-efficacy are likely to be more confident about their capabilities and more motivated to sustain their efforts when faced with challenges. Bandura suggested that there were four key ways in which individuals could build self-efficacy.

1. By *mastery experiences* which involves approaching life with dedicated effort towards realistic and challenging goals. According to Bandura: *resilient efficacy requires experience in overcoming obstacles through perseverant effort. Success is achieved by learning from failed efforts* (2008, p2).

2. By *social modelling* which involves choosing role models as a source of inspiration and aspiration: *seeing people similar to oneself succeed with consistent effort, raises the observers' beliefs in their own abilities to succeed* (ibid.).

3. By *social persuasion*, suggesting that if others encourage us to believe in ourselves we are more likely to exert the effort required for success. But this isn't just a case of any other person; successful persuaders need to be knowledgeable and skilled and, according to Bandura, they do more than simply convey their faith:

They arrange situations for others in ways that bring success and avoid placing them prematurely in situations where they are likely to fail. They encourage judgment of success by self-improvement rather than by triumphs over others. Pep talks without enabling guidance achieve little.

(ibid.)

4. Finally, Bandura makes reference to *physiological state*, emphasising the importance of mood on judging efficacy, suggesting that: *efficacy beliefs are strengthened by reducing anxiety and depression, building physical strength and stamina, and changing negative misinterpretations of physical and affective states* (ibid., p3).

CASE STUDY

Rachel's journal

I don't know what to make of today … the lesson seemed to go well and the students behaved, in fact they seemed to enjoy the activities I had set for them; I guess I was lucky I got them on a good day. So they were great … but I am not sure what the Head of Department thought of me … I babbled at the beginning - I forgot about one of my objectives and had to go back to it and I went five minutes over on one of the activities so had to reshuffle the lesson plan - I bet she thinks I am really disorganised.

The feedback I got seemed to be OK; the Head of Department said that the students were lively (I wonder if she thought I should have controlled the activities more?) and she commented on how I adjusted the lesson (so I guess she has me labelled as someone who can't plan properly?). Then she said something really odd … that I needed to be mindful of the language I was using … I started to panic and thought that somehow bad language had slipped out, but then she said … the language you use in relation to yourself … apparently this is very negative. Oh dear, does this mean I now have a reputation for being negative?

The importance of language

According to Newberg and Waldman (2013), words help us to translate messages from others but also have the ability to form our reality in quite practical ways. Words, it is suggested, can actually shape how we perceive reality: *human brains like to ruminate on negative fantasies, and they're also odd in another way: they respond to positive and negative fantasies as if they were real* (2013, p27). If this is the case, is it possible that the words we choose have a significant influence on the ways in which we think and, in turn, how we feel about particular situations or even ourselves? In Rachel's case, it seems that all the positive feedback she was given was overwhelmed by her own negative thoughts, even the very constructive advice provided by her Head of Department who suggested she should think about the language she used in relation to herself.

Research linked to the connection between language and thought suggests that there is also a relationship between these characteristics and our feelings. Butler and Hope cite experiments carried out with patients suffering from anxiety who, when calm and at ease, were asked to read out loud certain word pairs. *If their list of words contained pairs such as 'breathless-choking' or 'palpitations-dying'* *they experienced sudden and intense waves of anxiety and started to panic* (2007, p74). This research was used to demonstrate how thoughts, prompted by language, in turn influenced our feelings. As illustrated by Figure 10.2, this is something which could quite naturally turn into a depressed or anxious cycle.

Figure 10.2 Downward spiral

Strategies for developing resilience

What is it that makes some people more resilient than others? Often resilience is described as a personal characteristic and we may view a particular person as being resilient or not. On this basis it is easy to assume that this is inherent and not necessarily something we can develop, but some sources suggest that we can in fact learn to develop our resilience and build this into everyday life.

Grit

Duckworth refers to 'grit' as a positive trait linked to a person's perseverance in relation to achieving a goal (Duckworth, 2016). This type of perseverance promotes the overcoming of obstacles and provides a motivational force towards achievement. This could be likened to the earlier definitions of resilience which relate to a certain attitude to overcoming the challenges that may block our progress. However, resilience itself is something we require to manage our day-to-day lives and is something we all have to a greater or lesser extent, whereas, grit, it seems, specifically relates to the passion and perseverance required for achievement. Developing grit, has been linked to five key areas.

1. Pursuing things which interest you – when focussing on goal achievement this may seem obvious but what about when this applies to our day-to-day roles? Most people are not interested in every aspect of their job, so the key here would be to balance elements of the job you don't like (for example completing administrative tasks) with the things you do like (perhaps preparing resources). My strategy here is to 'reward' myself by spending an hour or so on things I enjoy after I have completed a certain number of less enjoyable tasks.

2. Practice – it is no surprise to learn that to become good at something we probably need to practise, but an important focus here is to work on things we might consider 'weaknesses'. This echoes some of Bandura's (2008) ideas in relation to building efficacy and is similar to the work of Ericsson et al. (1993) who advocated improvement through 'deliberate practice'. Deliberate practice referred to the activities which were considered to be most effective in improving performance, therefore it is purposeful and systematic practice rather than just repetition. If we want our practice to be developmental, it is first important to highlight things which could improve, then compare these with 'expert practice' in this particular activity.

3. Finding purpose – having a defined purpose for our activities certainly makes them more motivating and this is very much linked to the first point. Interesting and purposeful activities are certainly more likely to inspire further practice.

4. Having hope – this doesn't refer to hope in terms of wishing, but in terms of taking a positive approach. We have hope because we have confidence that we are going to make something happen.

5. Joining a group – the final point relates to gaining support from like-minded people, so, in this case, the group will also be 'gritty'. By spending time with people who have a purposeful and positive approach to activities, we are more likely to be energised towards our own endeavours. You may have come across the idea that you are the sum of the five people you spend the most

time with (usually accredited to motivational speaker Jim Rohn); this may be a simplistic view but there is evidence to suggest that our social networks have a significant influence on our lives (Christakis and Fowler, 2011). After all, the people we spend time with have an impact on our experiences, our opinions and often how we feel about ourselves. So, if we want to achieve something specific, spending time with like-minded and potentially supportive people does seem to make a lot of sense.

PAUSE POINT

Look back at the five points related to developing grit and think about where Rachel might be going wrong.

CASE STUDY

Rachel's journal

I have been thinking a lot about the feedback on my lesson observation and had another look at the notes today. Actually, there are a lot of positives there; I don't know why I didn't notice that at the time. I had a long chat with a colleague today and we talked about this. She was really supportive and said she used to feel the same way because she got herself into a panic about other people making judgements on her teaching. She also mentioned using something called 'peer observation' where a colleague, rather than a manager, sits in on your lesson and then discusses things that were good or could be improved. I really like this idea; it somehow feels less scary and I think I might listen a bit more to the feedback ... I am definitely going to try it.

Characteristics of resilient people

According to Grant and Kinman (2013), emotional resilience might be described as the ability to recover from adversity when things become difficult and they stress the importance of using appropriate strategies to do so. These strategies include some of the things we have already discussed such as optimism, self-efficacy and good support networks, but also include reflection, self-awareness and a commitment to self-care and a work–life balance. All of these are practical approaches to developing day-to-day coping skills.

As suggested in this chapter, we can learn to take a more optimistic approach which will help us to find strategies to overcome the challenges we are faced with. While I certainly agree with this, I also think there are differences between *constructive optimism*, which could be seen as a strategy for moving away from set-backs, and *blind optimism* whereby we might simply be choosing to think positively without addressing or thinking through the initial obstacles. We can't simply resolve to be or do something and then continue to do exactly the same things. In order to make a difference we need to know what to change and take definite steps to make those changes. A blind optimism approach could actually make us less resilient, as by choosing not to directly address our concerns we are simply putting them aside and, in all likelihood, will trip up over them at a later date.

A more effective way of improving our resilience would be by developing our emotional intelligence, as this provides a 'safe' forum to explore how we think and feel about events or interactions in an objective way. Being emotionally intelligent simply means being in touch with our emotions and being able to accept them for what they are (i.e. emotions, not truths, facts or laws). This, in turn, allows us to be more flexible in our approach to situations. When we accept an emotion for what it is we remove much of its power and provide the space to view situations much more objectively. This is certainly a more effective approach than telling ourselves to be positive (and perhaps crossing our fingers or holding our breath for good luck).

Negative thoughts

This should include your negative thoughts about the situation.

Against each one include a rating of between 0–100.

e.g. 'The students were really noisy in that observation – I wasn't in control' – 60.

Distortions

Here you identify any potential distortions in thinking.

e.g. 'The lesson did seem to run smoothly, so I must have had some control.'

Rational responses

This is a space to substitute more objective thoughts.

Against each one include a rating of between 0–100.

e.g. 'The students were really noisy, this could be because they were enjoying the activity' – 80.

> *Now review how much you believe the original thought*

Figure 10.3 The Three Column technique (adapted from Burns, 1999)

Another key part of increasing resilience is to develop our capacity to manage challenges or deal with difficult situations. Most approaches to this involve clearly stating the issue or concern, then outlining ways of dealing with it. There are many strategies which could be employed here, depending on the nature of the situation; for example, if we are addressing a practical issue we might complete a mind map to explore its elements, then outline some specific strategies which will help us deal with it. Where the issue or concern is less practical and perhaps relates to something less tangible, like how we feel about something, we may need to consider an approach which allows us to reframe our thoughts and/or feelings. One strategy which could help in this instance is using a model of reflection and reframing. Burns (1999) suggests an approach referred to as the *four steps to happiness*. This is based on a model of reflection and analysis which highlights automatic thoughts and any distortions in thinking. In practice this would work by following these four steps:

1. identifying the situation;

2. recording your negative feelings about the situation;

3. using the triple column technique to tune into automatic thoughts, feelings and distortions;

4. then reviewing how much you believe in the automatic thoughts originally specified.

It is a simple approach to enhancing objectivity in our thinking by neutralising emotional responses. The triple column technique involves creating a table to include the areas outlined in Figure 10.3 on the previous page.

CASE STUDY

Rachel's journal

I had a peer observation today – what a revelation! My colleague sat in on the whole lesson and then at the end we spent about half an hour discussing it. She was really excited by some of the strategies I used and asked if I would mind sharing those with her. I was so flattered ... Imagine doing something that an experienced colleague actually wants to adopt. Interestingly ... I also got the same feedback about the way I use language and now I finally understand what this means. I do tend to panic and then beat myself up when things don't go perfectly. This certainly starts a negative spiral and sometimes I forget all the good stuff that has happened. I need to remember that sometimes things don't go particularly well but this doesn't automatically mean it's a personal reflection on me. It is quite an ingrained habit, but today I was introduced to a strategy to help with this using a series of simple steps which include honestly reflecting on my thoughts and questioning them. It has really helped me to be more objective. It is like a window has been opened and the whole room has been flooded by light. Amazing! In fact, this has been such a revelation I am going to think about ways I can help others to do the same thing. I did notice that a lot of my students seem to have the same problems in terms of being hypercritical of themselves and then getting really upset about things. There must be things I can do to help them to think differently about this ...

Helping others to develop resilience

Rachel has clearly had a revelation in terms of managing her own emotional responses to events and, in turn, being able to reframe them in more objective ways. This is certainly a skill that can help all of us to both manage set-backs and pursue particular goals; it is also something which can help us to support other people in developing their own capacity for resilience.

Much of the content in this chapter can be applied to students as well as teachers and the key aspects of resilience such as self-efficacy, persistence and emotional intelligence remain the same. But how do we include this type of activity in our lessons in ways which don't remove the focus from the subject we are teaching? There are a number of strategies which are based on the underpinning theories we have already explored.

- Making connections – finding opportunities to make connections with others can be included into most classroom settings through the use of collaborative learning. This can be particularly helpful if these activities are based on agreed rules in relation to working together in positive ways.

- Creating a constructive learning environment – encourages co-construction of knowledge. This is useful for showing that there is rarely one way of doing something, an idea which can be transferred to all areas of life. By allowing students to explore topics, you are also providing a space in which they can get used to problem-solving which is a key skill in building resilience.

- Viewing problems as challenges – this may be centred around motivation towards tasks and creating a sense of excitement around finding out answers. Scenarios, stories and case studies can also be used effectively to enhance this skill.

- Including change regularly – while there is an argument for having a solid structure in classrooms, if we don't introduce change we may also be limiting students' abilities to work effectively in different environments. Introducing and discussing change also reinforces that this is an important aspect of life and something we all need to cope with.

- Using individual goals and targets – this provides the scope to work individually with learners and discuss their approaches to particular activities. It also demonstrates that there are actions we can take towards overcoming challenges or achieving new things, which in turn helps to build self-efficacy.

- Encouraging reflection – this can be done by getting students to reflect on their own learning and their approaches to particular activities. It also helps to maintain perspective; by encouraging objective and honest reflection it is much easier to see things in context and not as being personal to the individual.

- Nurturing a positive view of self and others – this can be achieved by using peer- and self-assessment and feedback to encourage honest reflection on what we and others have been able to achieve.

Many of the suggestions above are effective teaching strategies which you may already be using so it isn't necessary to make any dramatic changes. The only difference here is that the focus may be on the development of interpersonal and affective skills rather than cognitive ones. The strategies themselves remain the same.

Chapter summary

The importance of resilience is now widely recognised as a factor of success; not only that, it is essential in the maintenance of mental health and well-being. In this chapter we have explored the meaning of resilience and how this can be applied to our working lives. We have also considered a range of strategies which can be used to develop our own resilience as well as that of others.

MENTOR MOMENT

In this section we have included starter points for discussions with mentors so that you can talk through the chapter content. The aim of the questions is to encourage you to interrogate your understanding of the concepts presented and consider ways in which these might influence your teaching.

- What does resilience mean to you?
- Are there times when you are more (or less) resilient?
- What strategies could you use to help build your own resilience?
- In what ways could you help students to develop their resilience?

Suggested further reading

Butler, G and Hope, T (2007) *Manage Your Mind: The Mental Fitness Guide* (2nd ed). Oxford: Oxford University Press.

Lakoff, G and Johnson, M (2003) *Metaphors We Live By*. London: University of Chicago Press.

References

Bandura, A (2008) An agentic perspective on positive psychology, in Lopez, SJ (ed) *Positive Psychology: Expecting the Best in People*. Volume 1. New York: Praeger.

Buchanen, GM and Seligman, MFP (1995) *Explanatory Style*. Hillsdale, NJ: Erlbaum.

Burns, DD (1999) *The Feeling Good Handbook*. New York: Plume.

Butler, G and Hope, T (2007) *Manage Your Mind: The Mental Fitness Guide* (2nd ed). Oxford: Oxford University Press.

Christakis, NA and Fowler, JH (2011) *Connected: The Amazing Power of Social Networks and How They Shape Our Lives*. London: Harper Press.

Clance, P and Imes, S (1978) The imposter phenomenon in high achieving women: dynamics and therapeutic intervention. *Psychotherapy Theory, Research and Practice*, 15 (3): 1–8.

Duckworth, A (2016) *Grit: The Power of Passion and Perseverence*. New York: Scribner.

Ericsson, KA, Krampe, RT and Clemens, T-R (1993) The role of deliberate practice in the acquisition of expert performance. *Psychological Review*, 100 (3): 363–406.

Grant, L and Kinman, G (2013). 'Bouncing back?' Personal representations of resilience of student and experienced social workers. *Practice: Social Work in Action*, 25 (5). Available at **https://doi.org/10.1080/09503153.2013.860092**

Health and Safety Executive (2018) Work related stress depression or anxiety statistics in Great Britain, 2018. Available at **www.hse.gov.uk/statistics/causdis/stress.pdf** (Accessed 13 April 2019).

Lakoff, G and Johnson, M (2003) *Metaphors We Live By*. London: University of Chicago Press.

Macsinga, I and Nemeti, I (2012) The relation between explanatory style, locus of control and self-esteem in a sample of university students. *Science Direct*, 33 (25): 29.

Newberg, A and Waldman, MR (2013) *Words Can Change Your Brain: 12 Conversation Strategies to Build Trust, Resolve Conflict, and Increase Intimacy*. New York: Plume.

Seligman, M (2018) *Learned Optimism: How to Change Your Mind and Your Life*. London: Nicholas Brealey Publishing.

FINAL THOUGHTS

This book was written as a resource to help you develop a deeper understanding of education theories and how they relate to practice. Our intention was to offer this information in a way which would allow you to personalise it so that you could take away some very practical ideas and ultimately improve your teaching and your students' learning. This isn't something you can do by simply following someone else's 'hints and tips' about teaching. Teaching, like learning, is a very personal thing and as such we need to think carefully about our approach to it.

The stories in this book outlined a range of issues we might encounter and demonstrate that we each interpret and manage these events in different ways, sometimes using several strategies to do so. This is exactly as it should be. Teaching is a relational skill and, as with all aspects of human relations, it is also something which must be individualised to both teachers and learners. To do this effectively we need to be flexible in our approach to how we interpret situations and what strategies we might employ to manage them. Theories and stories provide us with the information we need to do just that. But it doesn't end there ... for teaching to develop, we all need to continue learning; this means thinking about our approach, seeking out alternatives and continuing to strive to be the best we can be.

Einstein is famous for stating that he wasn't really more intelligent than other people but that he simply *stayed with the problems longer*. It is an important message for us all and we would add that problems can be transformed if you simply take the time to view them from different lenses. It is as much about having an open mind and being persistent than anything else. With that in mind, we return to another of Einstein's famous quotes ... *Life is like riding a bicycle. To keep your balance you must keep moving.* Enjoy the ride.

INDEX